WORLD DRESS
FASHION IN DETAIL

WORLD DRESS
FASHION IN DETAIL

ROSEMARY CRILL, JENNIFER WEARDEN
AND VERITY WILSON

WITH CONTRIBUTIONS FROM ANNA JACKSON AND CHARLOTTE HORLYCK

PHOTOGRAPHS BY RICHARD DAVIS
DRAWINGS BY LEONIE DAVIS

V&A PUBLISHING

Acknowledgements The authors would like to thank their V&A colleagues Clare Browne, John Clarke, Frances Franklin and Susan North for their advice.

First published by V&A Publications, 2002, as *Dress in Detail from Around the World*. Support for the first edition was provided by Asian Art in London.

This edition published 2009

V&A Publishing
Victoria and Albert Museum
South Kensington
London SW7 2RL

Distributed in North America by Harry N. Abrams, Inc., New York

ISBN 978 1 85177 568 2
Library of Congress Control Number 2008937538

10 9 8 7 6 5 4 3 2 1
2013 2012 2011 2010 2009

V&A Publishing
Victoria and Albert Museum
South Kensington
London SW7 2RL
www.vam.ac.uk

A catalogue record for this book is available from the British Library.

New cover design: Lizzie B Design
Designer: Area
Photographs: Richard Davis, V&A Photographic Studio
Drawings: Leonie Davis

Front cover illustration: Woman's tunic of embroidered silk, China (Xinjiang Autonomous Region), 19th or early 20th century. T.31c–1932 (see p.28).

Back cover illustration, left: Woman's *kimono* of woven silk, lining of woven silk and embroidered silk crepe, Japan, second half of the 19th century. T.78–1927 (see p.136);
right: Woman's dress (*sarafan*) of silk satin brocaded with metal thread and cotton, Northern Russia, second half of the 19th century. 549–1907 (see p.44).

Inside cover illustration: Man's robe of cotton embroidered with wool, Northern Nigeria (Hausa), early 20th century. Circ.125–1966 (see p.126).

Frontispiece: Detail from woman's sleeveless coat, Montenegro, c.1850. T.321–1921 (see p.200).

Printed in Singapore by C.S. Graphics

Contents

Introduction

The garments in this book reflect the exceptional range of the Victoria and Albert Museum's dress collections. The clothes come from many different countries. However, not every country, or even every continent, is represented here and we make no claims to anything approaching a comprehensive survey of world dress. Historically, the arbitrary division of artefacts into either ethnography or art means, for example, that there are not many garments in the V&A from the continent of Africa and none at all from Oceania. Britain's complex colonial past together with individual curatorial preferences and chance acquisitions over the years have further defined the world dress collections, parts of which are as old as the Museum itself. The first dress items to enter the V&A early in its history were not from dominant western nations at all but rather from diverse cultures spread across the globe. The Museum is particularly rich in Asian, Middle Eastern and Eastern and Central European garments but, until fairly recently, this singular collection was not necessarily perceived in terms of dress. Some of these clothes were acquired for their interesting fabrics and for the opportunity they presented for studying a wide range of different textile techniques, as well as designs, used in their decoration.

This book, while neither primarily about technique nor about design motifs, in some measure will be a resource for both since they are inseparable from the discussion of detail which we offer here. These details, illustrating diverse solutions to both the making and wearing of clothes, are enhanced by line drawings showing the whole garment's construction. The drawings and details dispel any residual assumptions concerning the supposed simplicity of indigenous garments, for they offer up inventive ways to control and assemble cloth. For example, panels and gussets may be arranged to enhance the drape of the garment or to use up left-over fabric, multifarious finishing techniques might strengthen the clothes while adding unique decorative focal points, and pockets and fastenings can be fashioned and placed to ensure modesty and personal temperature control. We have chosen to lay out the material according to garment feature rather than group it by region, date, type or use. Other books in the series are arranged in a similar manner although they are concerned with narrower bands of western fashion and limited to a specific time span. This present volume provides an opportunity to peruse the collection sliced in an unfamiliar way and such a perspective raises many valuable questions about clothing cultures across time and geography. The answers that tailors throughout the world have come up with, as exemplified by these garment details, are sometimes unique to their culture alone and sometimes shared with other cultures. All can be viewed as inventive variations on a theme.

The clothes on the pages that follow, as well as emanating from a variety of places around the globe, also come from different eras. Few of them pre-date the nineteenth century – the hundred years that saw élites in several of the areas under discussion embracing either complete or partial western dress while their poorer compatriots sometimes had the style foisted on them. Indigenous dress itself has always been open to all sorts of influences both from near neighbours and from those further afield, so we cannot say anything about the origins of certain aspects of dress by looking only at the V&A's collection. Some of the pieces are contemporary. While this book is, in part, a celebration of indigo and madder, and a recognition of the beauty of hand-spun and hand-woven fabric, it also sets out to show that, while great swathes of the world may indeed be clad in T-shirts and jeans, there is a groundswell of people, local wearers as well as international designers, who continue to favour indigenous dress.

Moreover, they may re-work the older styles, sometimes with the aid of up-to-the-minute technology, into something new and vital, but still relevant to their own community.

We understand that footwear, headgear and other accessories are all part of the story of world dress but this has proved too large an area to include in this volume. Furthermore, the haphazard way the Museum's collections have been built up over the years means that complete ensembles were rarely collected. Despite this omission, what we are left with is abundant evidence of a truly remarkable cross-section of makers and consumers. Some of the clothes were made and worn in urban centres and some in rural outposts. Still others were made in one milieu for use in another. Ceremonial silks for performance and court ritual, necessitating large outlays of wealth, may seem far removed from cottons and linens decorated at home with braid and fringes for country weddings and we are aware of a certain awkwardness in juxtaposing such ensembles. We have given each item a national provenance regardless of the fact that many people in that country may not recognize it as their style of dress, for the Museum did not always record the clothing's precise regional source. What we can say though is that the pluralistic character of these varied garments should be seen as one of the V&A's dress collections great strengths. We celebrate diversity and difference and honour the women, men and children who made and wore these garments.
V.W.

Note:
Wherever possible, present-day names have been used for the countries and regions in which these garments were made.

Necklines

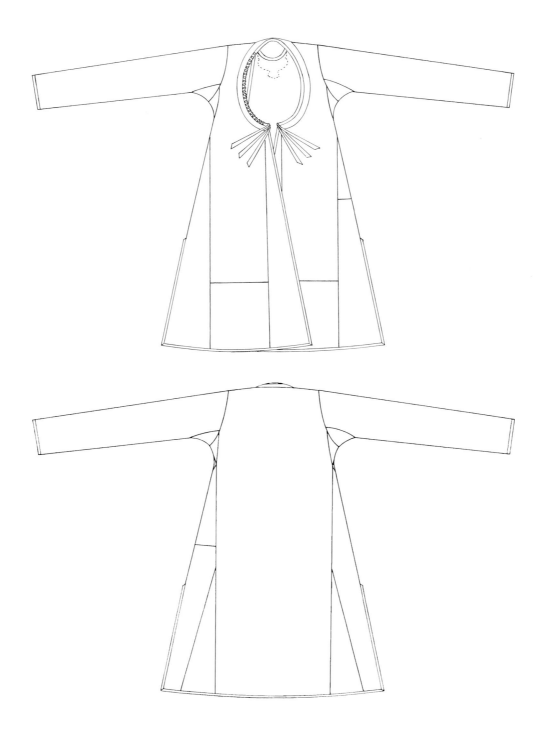

This luxurious robe is a courtly garment, worn by a young man in Sindh, Pakistan. It is made of silk and gold fabric, lined with red and yellow silk (see p.138 for the lining). The distinctive circular opening, combined with a rectangular panel to cover the chest, identifies this garment as an *angarkha,* which simply means 'protector of the body'. The upper part of the robe is evidently its focal point, and it is made more elaborate by the addition of a row of non-functional 'buttons' around one side of the front opening. Like all robes of this type, the distinctive round neck and waist are fastened by silk ties – in this case in red, blue and yellow – which are also used for the colourful piping around the neck and edges. It would have been paired with narrow trousers (*paijama*) of silk and gold fabric.

Man's robe (*angarkha*) of silk and metal thread
with applied ribbon and gold-wrapped 'buttons'.
Pakistan (Sindh), mid 19th century
05648 (IS)

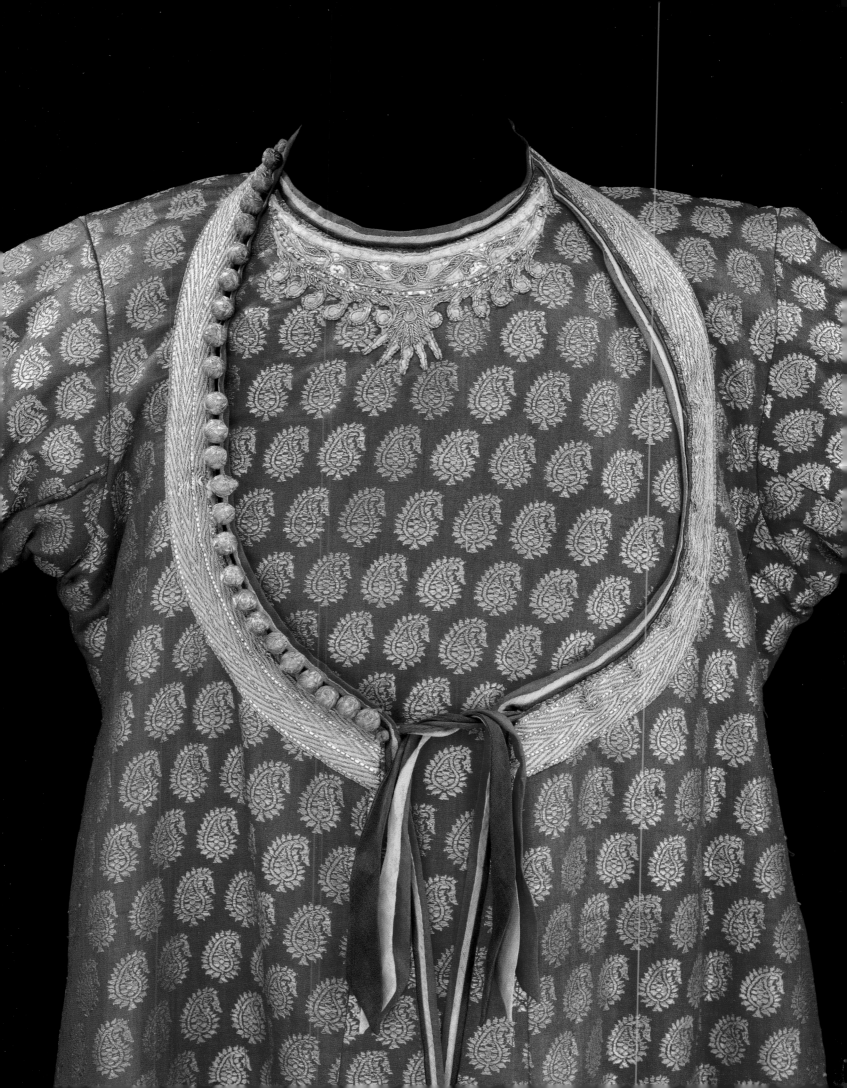

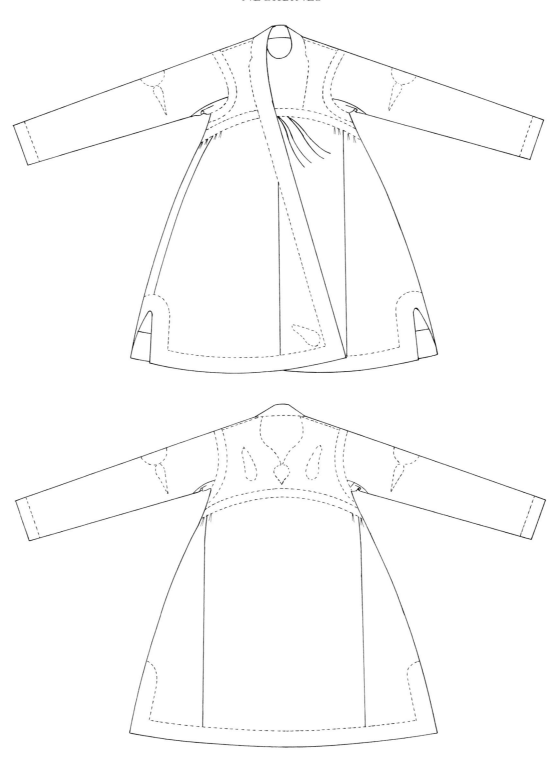

The distinctive side-fastening panel that passes over the chest of this young man's robe is typical of a type of *angarkha*. This panel is secured in two places inside the robe with green silk ties, and another pair keeps the waist closed. The robe is unusual in that it is made of the fine Kashmir wool more often associated with shawls. The intricate, spiralling pattern in couched gold-wrapped thread is typical of the work of Kashmir and of Panjab, where this coat would have been worn. Its lightly padded woollen material would have protected the wearer from the severe winters of these northern areas. The brilliant green silk ties are echoed in the neck-facing and lining of the same material.

Man's robe (*angarkha*) of red wool couched with gold-wrapped thread.
India or Pakistan (Kashmir or Lahore),
mid 19th century
05643 (IS)

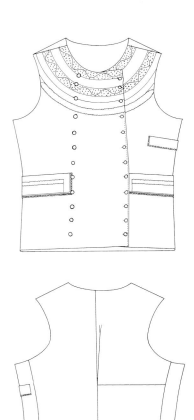

This was a wedding garment worn by a fisherman who, according to the man who sold it to the Museum, was later drowned at sea. It is made from black felt and is double-breasted, fastening either to the left or to the right.

Although the pockets are decorated with applied braid, it is the neckline that receives greatest attention. Two curving bands of black velvet have been applied to the felt and then decorated with cords and sequins, each held in place with a glass bead. Above and below the lower band is a series of lines worked in fine chain stitch. These red bands are slightly wider on the left-hand panel. Below them are lines of metal and silk braid and pink and yellow chenille – a tufted, furry yarn named after the French word for a caterpillar. Below these is an applied metal braid with more sequins. The fine coloured lines set against the black felt and velvet create a restrained and elegant effect.

Man's waistcoat of felt embroidered with
silk and trimmed with metal braid and sequins.
France (Department of Finistère), c.1820
16A-1902

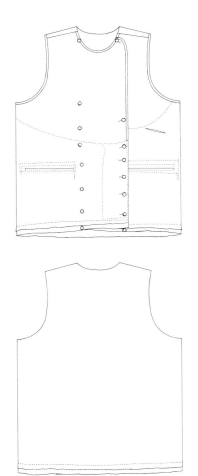

Solid spirals of golden silk decorate the neck of this waistcoat, which is made from black felt. Narrow strips of black silk velvet bind the armholes, the neck and the upper part of the front opening. It is double-breasted and can be fastened to the left or to the right, although most photographs of this type of garment being worn show it fastened right over left.

When fastened this way the full effect of the dense embroidery can be seen. The silk thread, which has faded slightly, was originally bright orange with small details worked in green. If fastened the other way – left over right – a different, less dense pattern is revealed which includes a series of narrow lines worked over wide strips of applied black silk velvet. The delicacy of the embroidered lines allows the velvet pile to show and is in sharp contrast to the strength that would have been required to take the silk thread through three layers of fabric: velvet, felt and canvas.

Man's waistcoat of felt with applied silk
velvet embroidered with silk.
France (Department of Finistère), late 19th century
Given by Mrs Goetze
T.25-1945

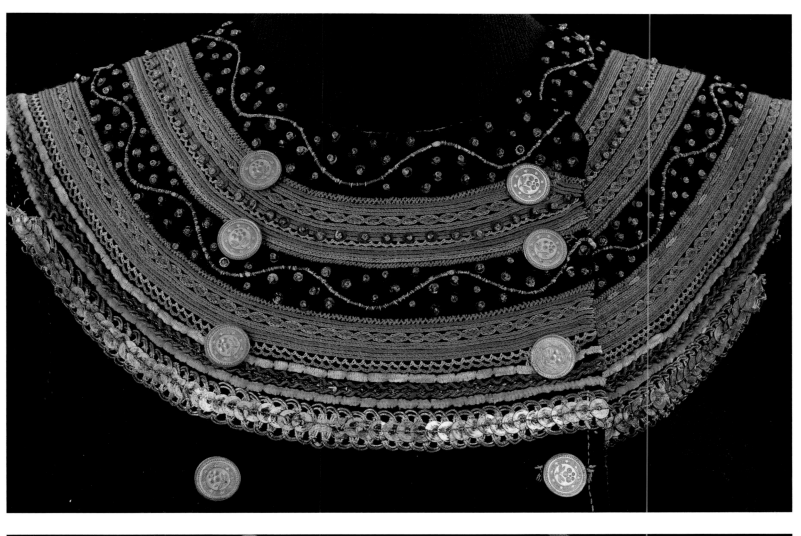

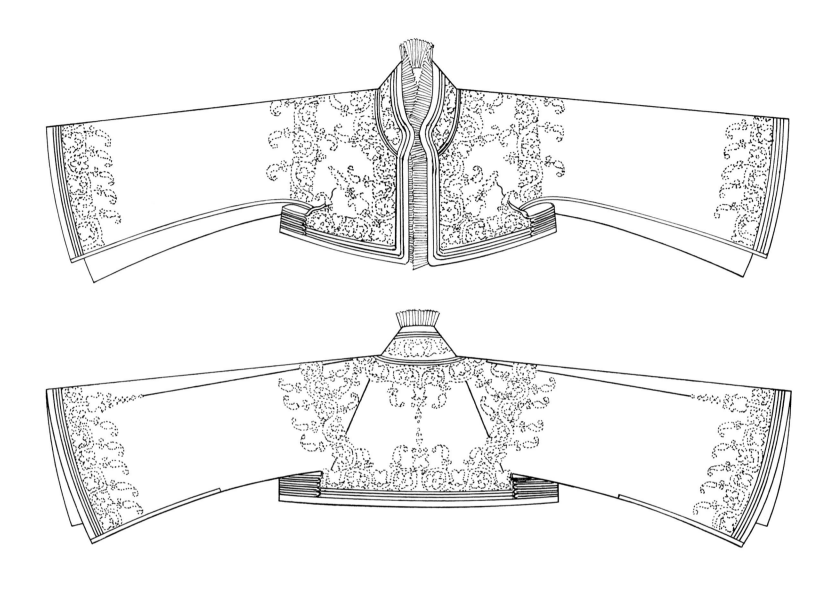

Velvet jackets, waistcoats and coats heavily embroidered with metal thread were part of formal dress in many areas of south-eastern Europe and the Near East from about 1830 onwards. They were influenced by the use of gold embroidery on military and diplomatic uniforms: the stiff, erect collar encrusted with gold and silver thread, which spills onto the front of this short jacket, has a distinct military bearing. The embroidery is restrained, following an undefined but obvious edge with only the occasional tendril extending across the bodice. Even these seem rigid and bound, weighted down by the addition of snaking threads and rings of silver cord.

The whiteness of the silver is picked up by a delicate ruffle of pleated silk chiffon, which has been attached around the collar and front edges. Its tiny pleats have knife-sharp creases but the transparent silk is soft and light and falls into ripples of gossamer as it caresses the neck. It is totally feminine and very unusual in a garment of this type. Although it has been securely attached, the quality of the stitching is poor which suggests it has been added by another hand – probably to make the jacket reflect western European fashion.

Woman's jacket of silk velvet embroidered
with metal thread and trimmed with silk chiffon.
Bosnia and Herzegovina, c.1880
Given by George Hubbard and purchased by him in 1884
T.178A-1928

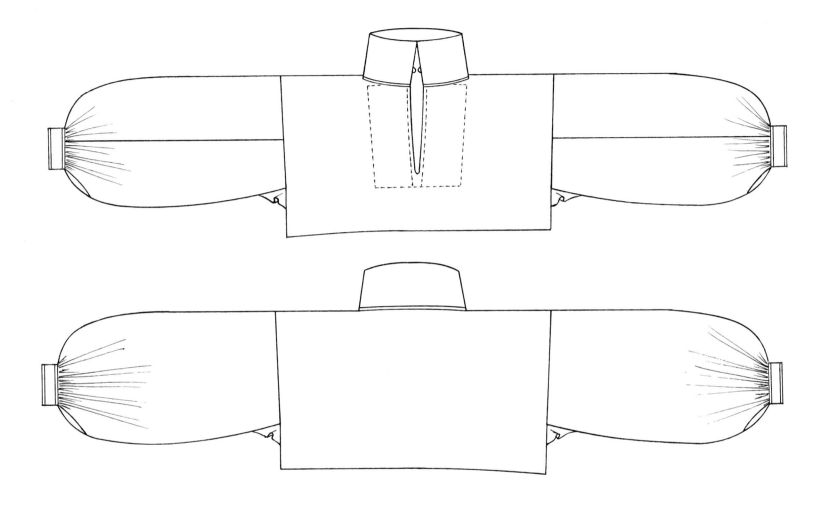

The cool climate of northern Europe makes it desirable to wear clothes that fit the body snugly at the wrist and neck in order to retain body heat. This high stand-up collar was made from two thicknesses of cloth, embroidered with wool in small and closely packed cross stitch, creating a substantial fabric with a fair degree of rigidity. It would have been secured with a piece of silver jewellery inserted through the two loops. Not only would the wearer's neck and shoulders have been kept warm, but the height of the collar would have required her to maintain her shoulders and head in an elegant, upright posture.

It is difficult to achieve a sharp, crisp edge at the bottom of a neck slit such as this. As the fabric is turned under and secured, there is a tendency for the slit to widen into a curve. In order to disguise this and to reinforce the part most vulnerable to tearing, a few interlacing stitches have been worked with blue wool.

Woman's blouse of cotton with linen sleeves embroidered with wool.
Norway (East Telemark), mid 19th century
Given by the Directors of the Museum of Art Industry,
Christiania (present-day Oslo)
797-1884

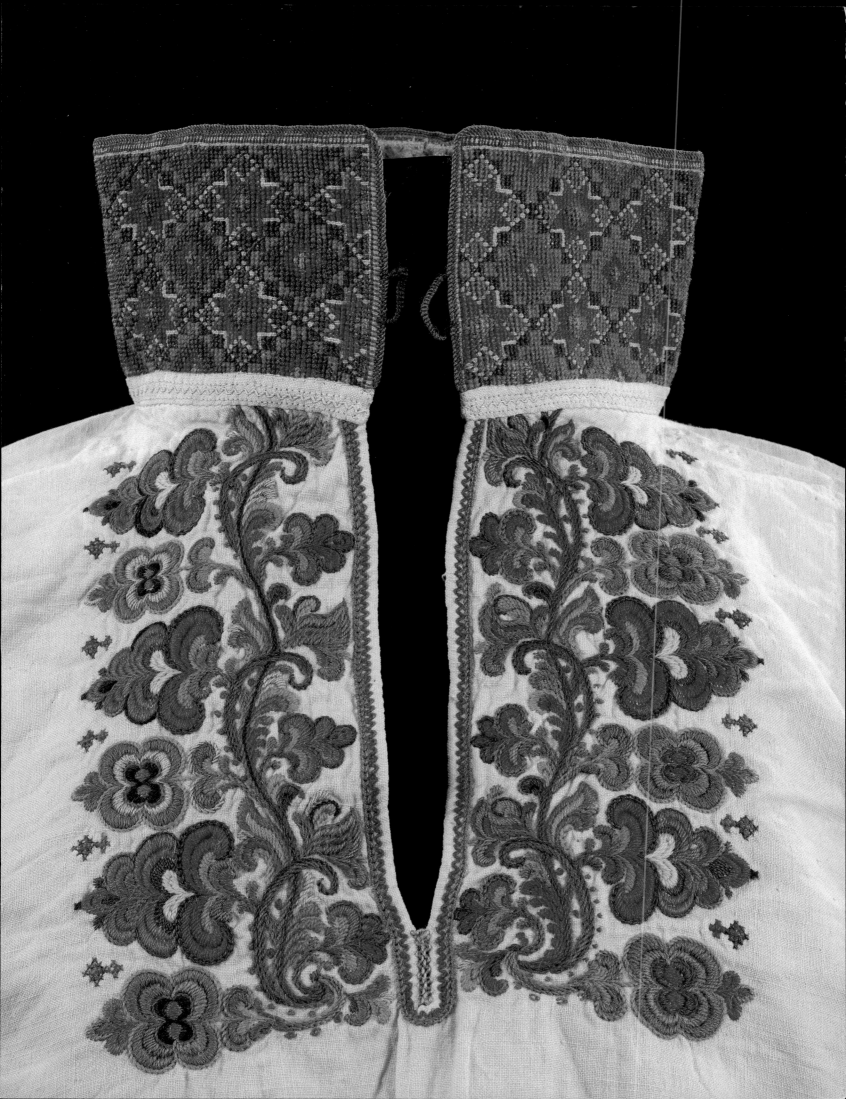

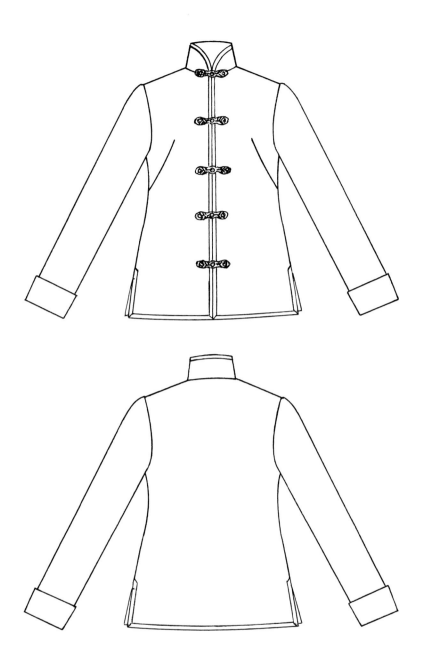

This short jacket was worn by the donor with black trousers and a matching top. She chose the turquoise velvet and her tailor suggested the olive green trim. Its unusual colouring gives it a unique and special look. The turquoise material has cut velvet motifs scattered across it, with the Chinese character for 'long life' matched across the front opening. The same design occurs on the lilac top on p.55. While both garments retain this traditional Chinese patterning on the material, neither of them is traditionally cut or tailored. The style of neckline on this jacket is sometimes perceived as being especially Chinese. Historic Chinese garments, however, do not invariably show this feature. It seems to have come into vogue in the years either side of 1900, perhaps reviving a much earlier style. Here, the high collar, rounded at the front, is stiffened and the entire jacket is lightly wadded to give it a crisp appearance when worn. A hook and eye beneath the top knot button secures the neck neatly. Plain velvet is used to bind the edges of the jacket and also to fashion the decorative froggings. These particularly strong components combine with the neckline to add to the garment's symmetry.

Woman's jacket of silk velvet.
China (Hong Kong), 1969
Given by Mrs Victoria Dicks
FE.45-1997

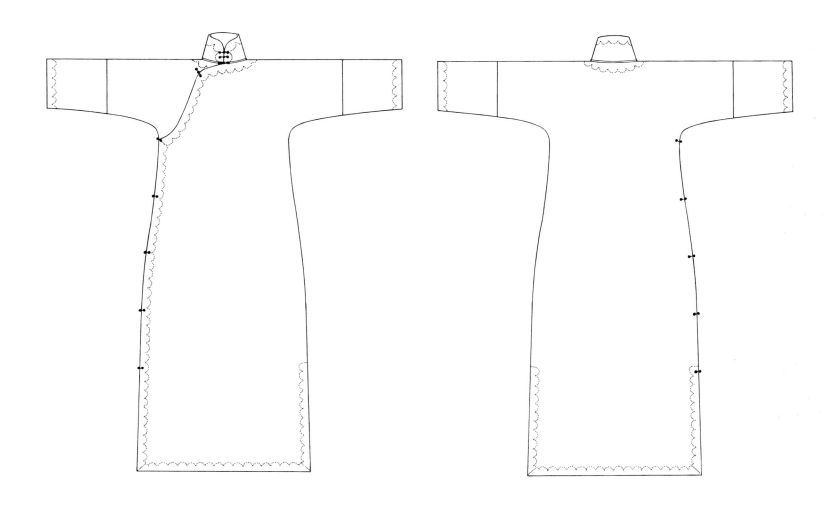

The exceptionally high neck on this dress is one of the features that particularly marks out the twentieth-century Chinese garment style known as the *cheongsam* or *qipao*. The neckband has a stiff interlining to ensure it stands upright when the dress is worn. A black lace trim has been sewn all around the neck and this frames the wearer's face. Black knot buttons and loops, arranged in a trio high up across the collar opening, further accentuate the neck and chin which would nestle into the space between the two sides of the neckband. Although attention might come to be focused on the wearer's head because of this concentrated decoration, the lace trim, an import from Europe, continues along the collarbone closure, down the side and across the hem and cuffs of the dress. This framing device harks back to the rows of trimming on women's gowns of an earlier period. While the trimming does not encroach much upon the main body of the garment, it may strike a traditional note on a dress that is far from traditional in its revelation of the female shape. Although the dress is full-length, it is tight fitting and has slits up the sides to reveal the legs.

Woman's dress (*cheongsam* or *qipao*) of printed satin.
China, 1930–40
Given by Christer von der Burg
FE.16-1994

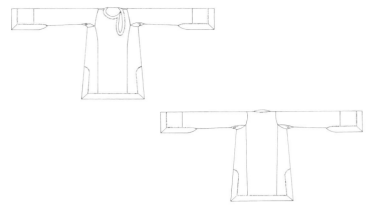

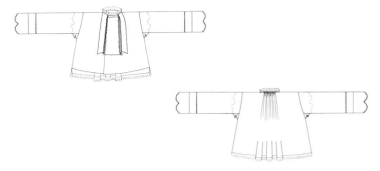

This fine cotton shirt is embroidered with a floral pattern in metallic embroidery, with more silver and gold edging around the neck, cuffs and hem. The design motif of bunches of grapes is composed of silver-gilt domed sequins and floss silk, while the heavy borders incorporate actual strips of flattened metal (see p.71). The shirt would have been worn over a small bodice (*choli*) in the same material, and a large, matching veil (*odhni*) would have been added over the head and shoulders. The ensemble would be completed by a full skirt, which has not survived. The off-centre neck opening of this shirt is a style found in rural as well as courtly garments, especially in the north and west of the Indian subcontinent.

Woman's shirt (*kurta*) of cotton, with silk and
metal embroidery.
Pakistan (Lahore), *c*.1855
6157 (IS)

Cleverly concealed beneath this construction of pin-tucks and embroidered panels are three large press-studs which fasten the blouse. Before the invention of the zip in the early 1890s, it was impractical to have garments which fastened down the back, and as women spent many years of their adult lives breast-feeding, a front-opening blouse made sense.

The three panels that have been attached to the bodice are examples of machine embroidery. The Schiffli embroidery machines were developed by Isaac Groebli in 1865 and could produce many varied effects, from simple eyelet embroidery to more complex patterns and structures such as these, which resemble certain types of lace. The subtleties of whitework are often overlooked but when textures are skillfully combined, as they are here, so that light is alternately absorbed and reflected, it is the epitome of elegance.

Woman's blouse of cotton with applied machine-embroidery.
Croatia (Sisak), late 19th or early 20th century
Given by Mr and Mrs C.O. Wakefield-Harvey
T.29A-1958

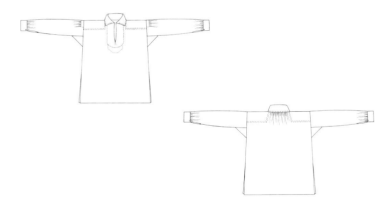

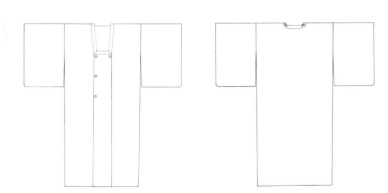

The Museum's collections contain very few garments from the Americas but this fine cotton shirt, so loosely woven that it is transparent, was acquired in 1854. It is from Paraguay and would have been worn over a pair of straight white cotton trousers, undecorated except for a fringe around the lower hem of each leg.

The double thickness of fabric used for the collar and the shoulders is embroidered with white cotton. The area to either side of the neck slit is decorated with pulled thread work in a pattern of leaves and blossoms. However, this is almost totally concealed by a flounce of embroidered net, which falls from below the single button fastening the collar. This surprisingly soft, feminine touch to a male garment is reminiscent of the lace cravats worn by fashionable men in western Europe in the first half of the eighteenth century.

Man's shirt of cotton embroidered with
cotton and trimmed with embroidered net.
Paraguay, *c*.1852
887-1854

This three-quarter length Japanese coat is a *michiyuki*, which literally means 'while on the road'. This style of women's outer garment developed in the twentieth century. It has a low, square neckline designed to reveal the *kimono* that would be worn underneath and it is fastened with six press-studs. Four fabric-covered buttons are sewn onto the front. The coat was created by Kitamura Takeshi who has studied and recreated one of the earliest, and most sophisticated, Japanese gauze-weaving techniques. It has a lattice pattern woven from silk thread, which was dyed before weaving with a vegetable dye derived from pomegranates. The fabric was woven in 1993 and made up into a *michiyuki* especially for the V&A in 1995, the same year that Kitamura was awarded the prestigious title of 'Living National Treasure'.

Woman's coat (*michiyuki*) of silk gauze (*ra*).
Japan, 1993–5
By Kitamura Takeshi (b.1935)
FE.274-1995

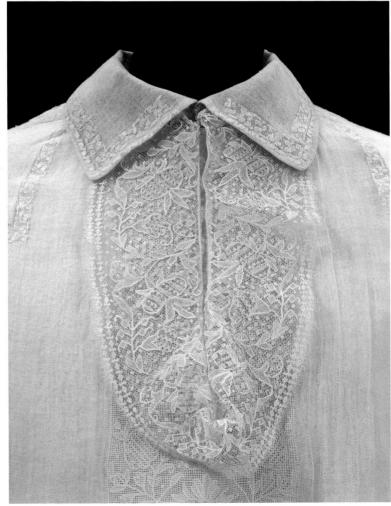

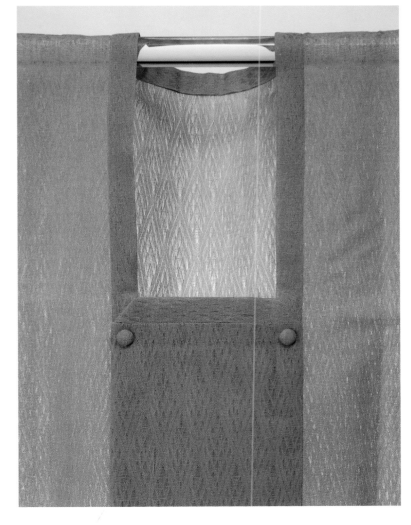

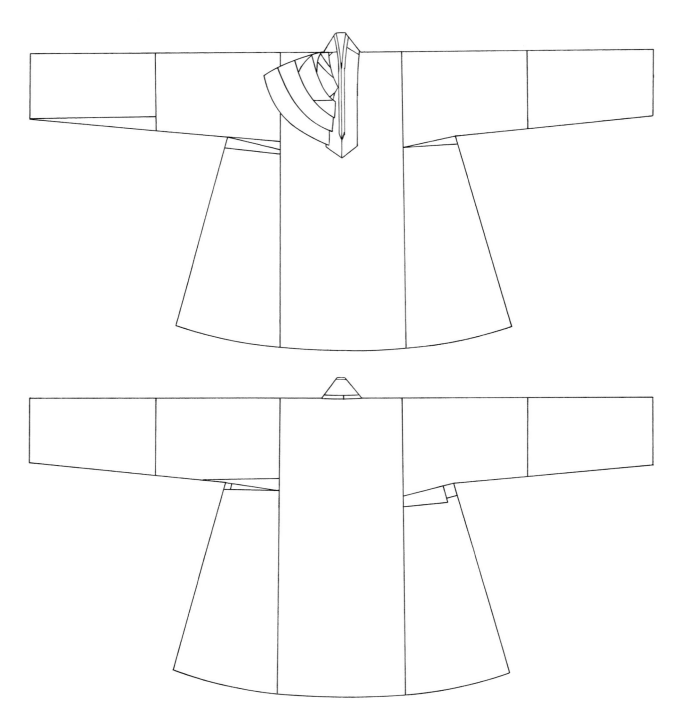

The asymmetric neck and shoulder decoration on this woman's tunic is composed of bands of patterned red and gold silk from India. Each strip was carefully teased into an arc shape as it was sewn onto the tunic. The section forming the collar is evenly gathered. This effect was achieved by inserting stiffeners secured by rows of stitching. The configuration of this applied decoration denotes that the wearer was a married woman. There are no fastenings to this tunic; the inflexible nature of the ruched neck prevents it from falling open. The tunic came into the Museum as part of a set with a magenta pink coat (see p.55), green trousers, red waistcoat, scarlet leather leggings, a tasselled hat and silver and coral plait decorations. George Sherriff (1898–1967), the renowned plant hunter who donated them to the Museum, recorded that he acquired them in Khotan, a town in today's Xinjiang Region of China. The likelihood is that the original wearer was from an ethnic group that today would be categorized as 'Uighur'.

Woman's tunic of embroidered silk.
China (Xinjiang Autonomous Region), 19th or early 20th century
Given by Captain George Sherriff
T.31c-1932

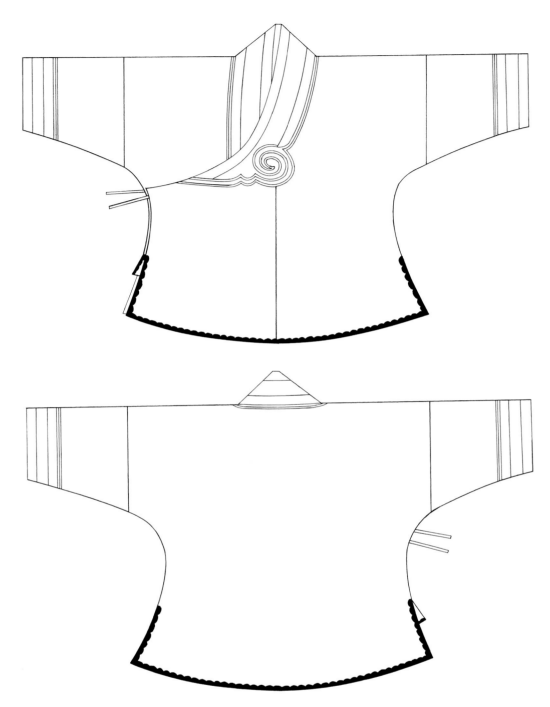

The collar band is beautifully shaped into a curl on the overlap section of this child's jacket. The embroidered white length of silk that forms the band is itself edged with narrower strips of ice-blue, bias-cut silk, which follow the curving outline. Similar edgings are applied around the cuffs. The jacket's tailoring, although similar to an adult's robe, differs from a full-size one in that the neckline shape is straighter and has no knot buttons across it. The method of closure is a tie at the side instead – a throwback to earlier Chinese fastenings. While the margins of the garment are pale, the main part of the jacket is a strong red: a colour associated in China with joyous occasions. It was the custom to present a young child with red and green clothes bearing good luck motifs. The gold-crowned figure in the centre depicts a male child bearing wishes for a son who will be successful in government high office. This jacket, part of a complete set, serves as a reminder not to read the Chinese decorative repertoire too literally. The garment was made by the Chinese neighbours of a European family, the Perriams, for their baby daughter in Shandong Province in North China in 1915.

Child's jacket of embroidered silk.
China (Shandong Province), 1915
FE.12-1986

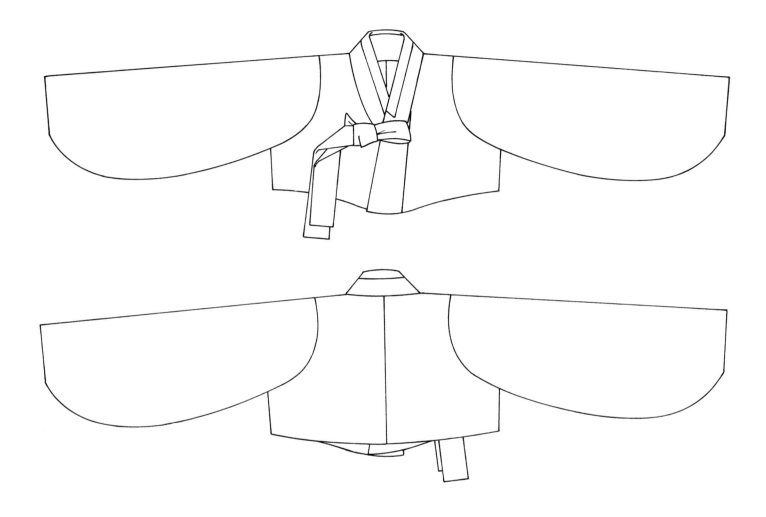

Yellow with a red collar and bow, this multicoloured jacket *(saek-tong jŏgori)* has striped sleeves in the five primary colours of blue, yellow, red, white and green, which can also be seen on the front of the jacket. As is customary with Korean jackets, the neckline is lined with a white border. Since this border can easily be taken off and washed or simply replaced, the neckline can be kept clean without difficulty and the jacket has a longer life-span. Here the border is made of the same material as the inner lining but con-temporary mass-produced ones are white. They are lined with paper in order to make them suitably stiff and durable. The red border has been decorated with an auspicious gold pattern of twenty-petalled chrysanthemums, frequently seen on children's costumes. There are different ways in which gold is applied to Korean tex-tiles. The unevenness of the flowers suggests that here a 'scatter gold' technique *(salgŭm)* was used. The pattern is first carved into a wooden mould and thereafter covered with glue. The cloth is then pressed into the mould, allowing the glue to seep through the material, and then gold powder is sprinkled over the wet glue.

Girl's jacket, woven silk.
Korea, mid 20th century
Given by Mr and Mrs D. Bebb
FE.114-1997

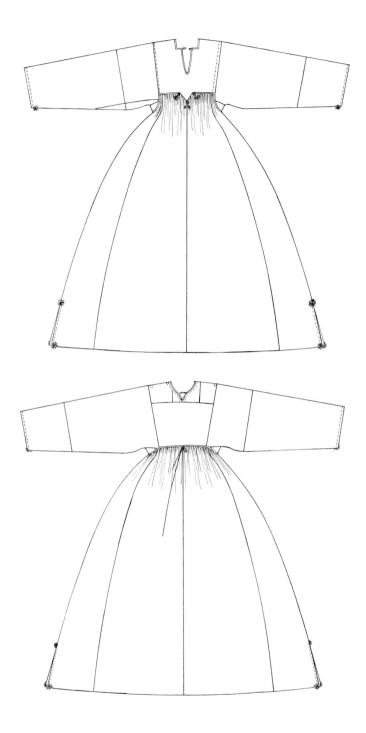

The dark indigo-blue cotton used for the main body of this dress, and many others in north-west Pakistan, is locally woven and dyed. While some dresses are made up solely in this rather austere material, others, like this one, are decorated, usually on the chest, with beautifully embroidered patterns, as well as with silk tassels and other embellishments. The small triangular element that hangs from the waistband of this dress is probably derived from a traditional amulet form, which protects the wearer and promises fertility. Such triangular amulets may be found in cloth or metal, and are seen very widely, especially on women's and children's dress, throughout Afghanistan, Muslim Central Asia and much of Pakistan.

Woman's dress of cotton with silk panels and silk embroidery.
Pakistan (Dera Ismail Khan, North-West Frontier Province),
mid 19th century
05603 (IS)

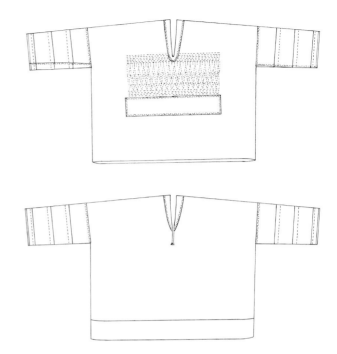

The simple V-shaped neck of this woman's garment is edged with imported woollen cloth, probably from Britain. Foreign fabrics were greatly prized in Burma, and this red wool is also used for a panel across the front of the black satin garment and for the sleeves. Its only other decoration is a panel of simple embroidery in silk threads below the neck opening. This shirt is part of a complete costume acquired in 1934 from a woman of Taungpeng, Northern Shan State in Burma. The rest of the outfit includes a skirt, apron, outer cape and separate sleeves.

Woman's shirt of satin with silk embroidery
and woollen panels.
Myanmar (Burma), (Palaung tribe, Northern Shan State),
early 20th century
Given by Mrs R.F.B. Lee
IM.37A-1934

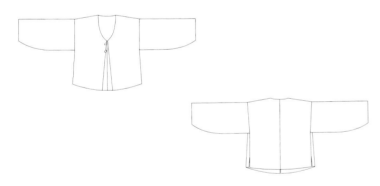

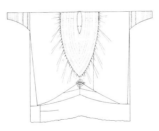

This Korean jacket was donated to the Museum by Yi Yong-hui, whose shop 'Hanall' in Seoul produces traditional Korean costumes, as advertised on the label. It forms part of a matching bridegroom's outfit, which in addition to this jacket consists of an overcoat, waistcoat, underjacket, undertrousers, leg ties, belt, boots and a hat. When worn, the off-white collar of the underjacket is clearly visible and with its diagonal, right-sided closure, it delicately contrasts with the oval neckline of the jacket. The jacket is closed in the front with two spherical buttons in gilded and enamelled metal openwork, which are decorated with longevity symbols. Korean costumes are normally tied with ribbons, buttons traditionally only being used on formal wear. Nowadays, buttons are also seen on men's, and occasionally women's, jackets and waistcoats worn on important occasions, such as weddings and birthdays.

Man's jacket of yellow-patterned silk with grey silk lining.
Korea, 1992
By Yi Yong-hui
Given by Yi Yong-hui
FE.542:2-1992

This dress is made from two layers of soft cotton extensively decorated with a series of embroidered bands covering the shoulders and chest and appearing to hang around the neck like a massive piece of jewellery. Only four colours are used and with such a limited palette pattern and texture are very important. The solid, flat bands of chevrons separate three chain-like patterns in which the ground fabric has been manipulated to form small bumps. The easiest way to achieve this effect is to pinch a small area of the cloth, wrap thread around the raised part and then outline the rows of bumps with embroidery.

The scale of the embroidery is in sharp contrast to the actual size of the neck and cuffs: each cuff, which is also decorated with embroidered bands, measures only 14cm (5½ inches) in circumference; the neck, which fastens with a silver button on the left of the image and a dark blue loop on the right, measures 27cm (10½ inches) in circumference. This dress was taken by British troops at the seige of Magdala (1868) and is said to have belonged to Queen Woyzaro Terunesh, the second wife of King Theodore.

Woman's dress (kamis) of cotton embroidered with silk.
Ethiopia, 1860s
Given by the Secretary of State for India
399-1869

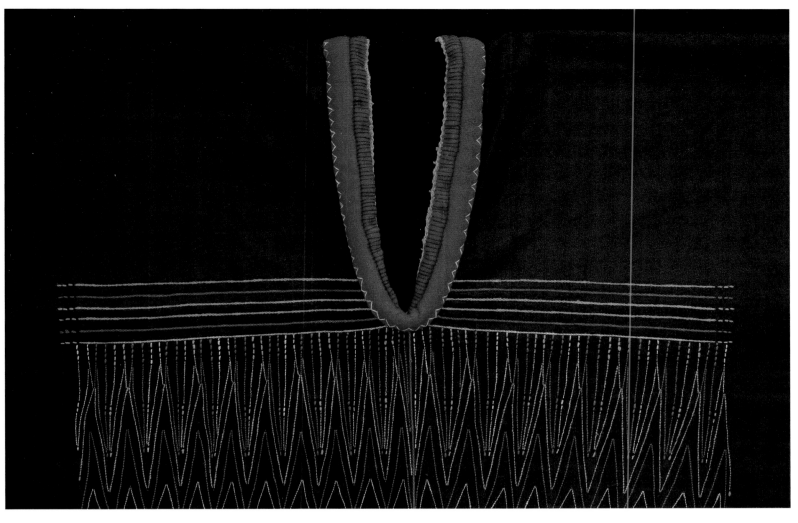

Fastenings

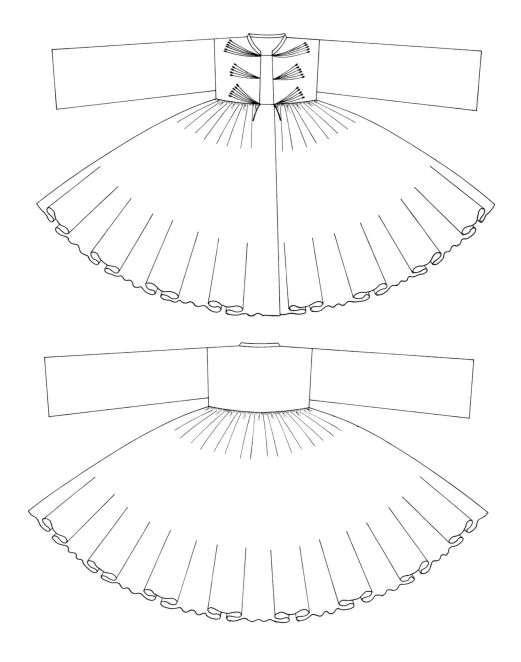

The three pairs of tassels on the front of this dress may or may not be intended as actual fastenings. A separate single pair of ties at the waist keeps it closed at that point, and a rectangular panel behind the tassels ensures that modesty is maintained whether or not they are tied. The tassels are carefully made of pieces of cotton cloth rolled into tubes and finished with embroidered red silk ends. White clothing is quite unusual in north-west Pakistan, where this dress comes from. Dark blue or black cotton is more frequently used for dresses and shirts, whether plain or embroidered.

Woman's dress of cotton embroidered with silk thread.
Pakistan, (North-West Frontier Province, probably Dera Ismail
Khan region), mid 19th century
05488 (IS)

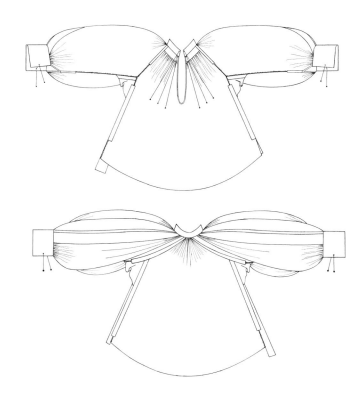

This collar is not as deep as it looks: only the upper part is actually an attached collar, the rest of it is a broad band of close decorative stitching on top of tight gathering.

Controlling the balloon-like fullness of this blouse was the main concern of the maker and so it is tightly gathered into embroidered cuffs and gathered all around the neck with its combination of formal, solid blackness and frivolous fastenings.

Three holes have been punched down the sides of the neck opening. A woollen cord has been threaded through each opposing pair and then a small pompom has been attached to either end of the cord. The top cord is the longest and the middle one is the shortest. When the collar is fastened tightly the upper and lower cords hang in graceful loops and the shortest cord adds bulk to the middle.

Woman's blouse of cotton embroidered with wool.
Hungary, c.1900
T.841B-1974

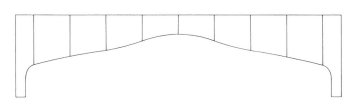

These beautifully patterned lappets are typical of the elegant robes (*jama*) worn by men at the Mughal and other Indian courts from the seventeenth to nineteenth centuries. The *jama* traditionally fastens at one side and is secured under the arm with ties. The ties were often made into a decorative feature, either by being in a contrasting colour or by being beautifully designed in their own right, as they are here. A simpler set of ties at the waist holds the robe closed. This robe fastens on the right, which traditionally denotes a Muslim wearer, with Hindus fastening their robes on the left. This practice, supposedly introduced by the Mughal Emperor Akbar (1555–1605), was not rigidly imposed or observed, but can serve as a useful aid when identifying subjects of court portraits.

Man's robe (*jama*) of cotton, mordant-dyed and printed.
Northern India, mid 18th century
Given by G.P. Baker
IS.110-1950

Trousers with immensely wide waists and narrow legs are traditional in many parts of the Islamic world, and this silk pair from Pakistan is an extreme example of the style. The waist measures a remarkable 9.15 metres (30 feet), and would form a huge bundle of cloth around the hips when the decorative drawstring (*ezarband*) is tightened. This drawstring is made using the sprang technique in silk, with bound metal-wrapped thread and silk expertly manipulated to form tassel-like ends. The trousers would probably have been worn with a loose straight shirt (*kurta*).

Woman's silk trousers.
Pakistan (probably Panjab), mid 19th century
05593 (IS)

In Korea the traditional dress (*hanbok*) for women consists of a short jacket and a long, voluminous skirt. Though the basic elements of the *hanbok* have essentially remained the same over a period of more than 1500 years, the length of the jacket and the fullness of the skirt changed over time according to fashion. The two ribbons used for fastening the garment in a front bow did not become a primary element of the jacket until the end of the Koryŏ period (AD 918–1392). Depending on fashion, the colour of the ribbons tends to offset that of the jacket, and often the cuffs and the neckline are lined with material identical to that of the ribbons, though this is not the case here. This jacket was made to be worn with the trousers on page 124.

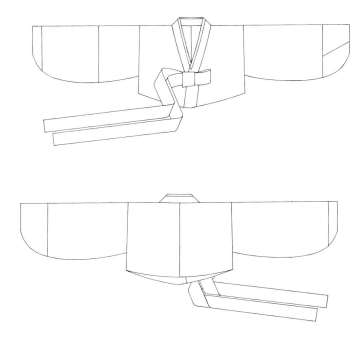

Woman's jacket of silk gauze.
Korea, 1995
By Chunghie Lee (b.1945)
FE.281:1-1995

It is unclear whether the brilliant green glass drops down the front of this man's robe are actually intended to be fastened, or whether they were meant to dangle purely as decoration. Each drop has a tiny loop at the end, which theoretically could connect with the corresponding loop on the facing strip of braid. This arrangement would require something to be threaded through all the loops to secure them, which would be not only a very fiddly operation, but would also tighten the upper part of the robe leaving an excess of fabric to be tied at the side of the waist. This unusual garment is a cross between an *angarkha* (which is fastened with ties) and an *achkan* (which has buttons down the front), and it appears that the tied mode of fastening is the more effective in this instance.

Man's robe of cotton with gold braid and green glass drops.
Pakistan (Sindh), mid 19th century
05620A (IS)

Accurately aligning buttons with the loops into which they fasten is tricky but when twenty-eight buttons had to be attached along the 112 cm (44 inches) front opening of this dress, a relatively quick and simple technique was used. Instead of sewing each button and its corresponding loop in place, a length of orange silk cord was threaded through the metal loop at the base of each shiny hollow brass or solid lead button. Once the buttons had been strung onto the cord, it would have been easy to stitch the cord along one edge of the front opening, spacing the buttons at regular intervals. A corresponding cord was stitched to the other edge, forming a loop opposite each button.

The colour of these cords has faded but was originally bright orange and because the silk is floss (untwisted), it was originally glossy and added to the shine and glitter of this dress.

Woman's dress (*sarafan*) of silk satin brocaded
with metal thread and cotton.
Northern Russia, second half of the 19th century
549-1907

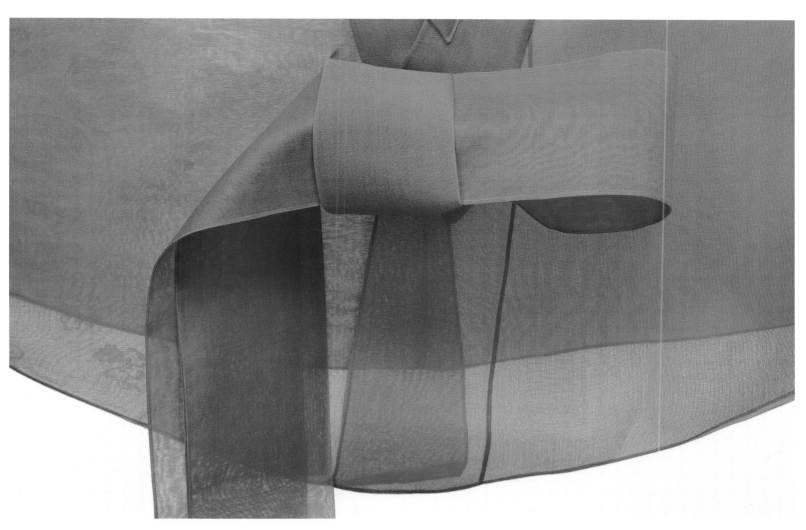

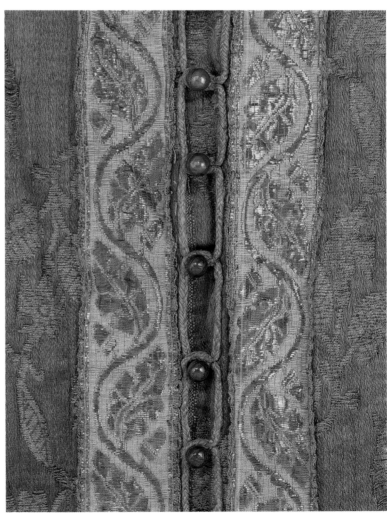

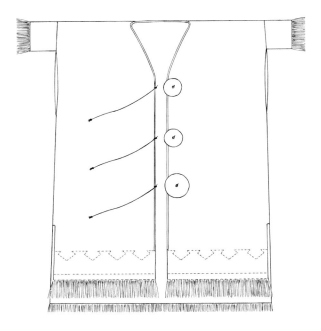

The designs on this jacket from Borneo relate closely to those on the intricately woven baskets from the same area, and are also found on local ikat-patterned and beaded textiles and garments. Here, the designs are woven and embroidered. The jacket is fastened at the front with three round buttons made out of conch shell. There are no buttonholes, which are a European feature: instead, a braided string is wrapped around the back of the button. The simple shape of the jacket, with small projecting shoulder-pieces, is also found in garments made of bark-cloth or other materials.

Young man's jacket of cotton with conch shell buttons.
Indonesia (Borneo, Dayak people), mid 19th century
4808 (IS)

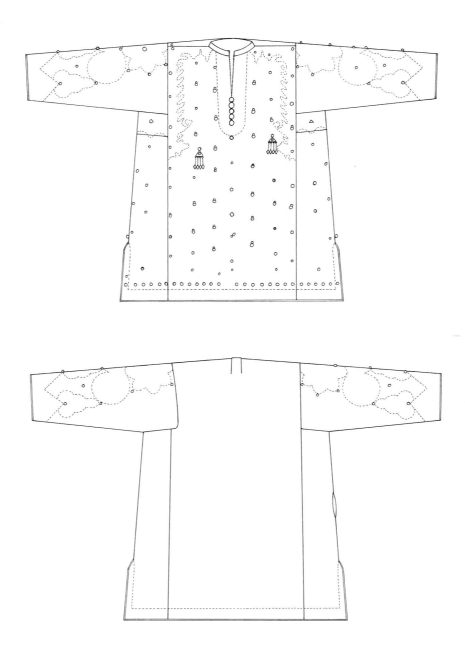

The zip-fastener used on the neck of this woman's shirt from northern Pakistan is unusual in that it is actually functional. Zips have gained great popularity in this remote area as a quick and easy way of applying a decorative trim to armholes and necklines, but are rarely used as closures. A traditional *kurta*, the form of shirt on which this one is based, would have a simple slit neckline with no actual fastenings, and the many buttons and press-studs that also appear on garments in this area are usually no more functional than the zips. This neckline is decorated with coins and plastic beads as well as embroidery, and the rest of the garment is also adorned with plastic and metallic embellishments. Their shapes suggest that many of them are based on jewellery forms but they have probably been purpose-made to be sewn onto clothing.

Woman's shirt (*kurta*) with embroidery and embellishments.
Pakistan (Indus Kohistan, North-West Frontier Province),
mid 20th century
IS.3-1997

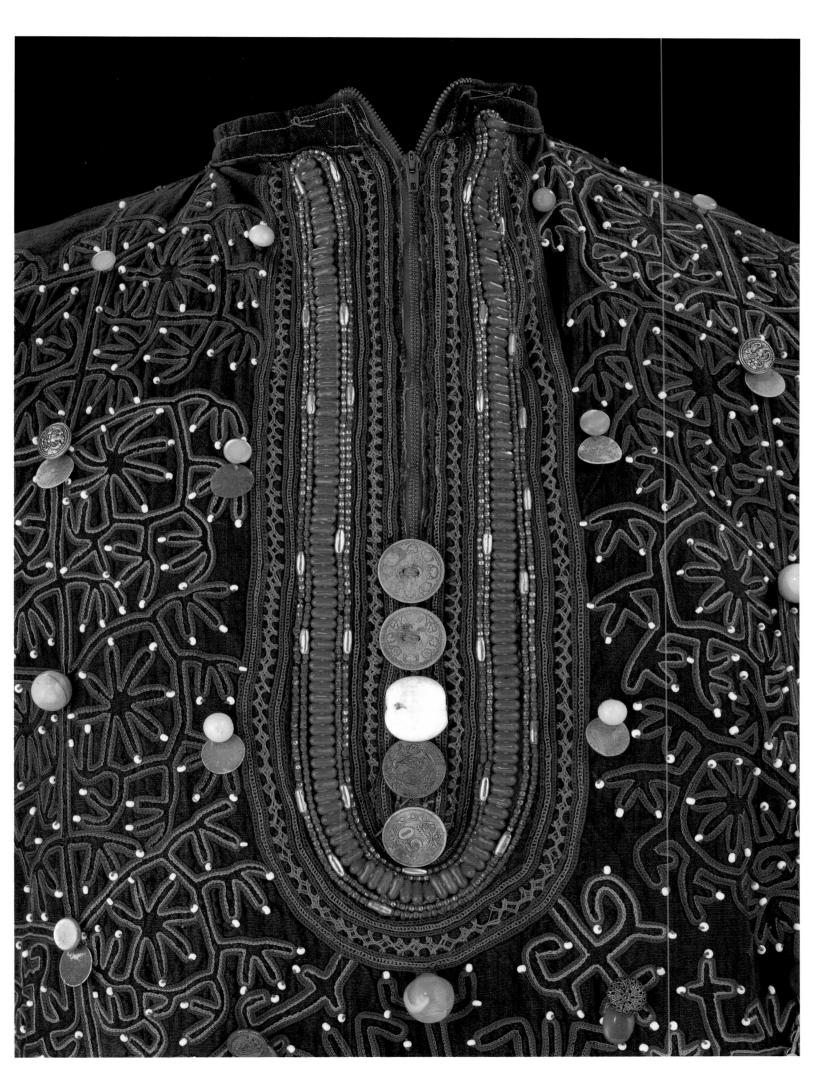

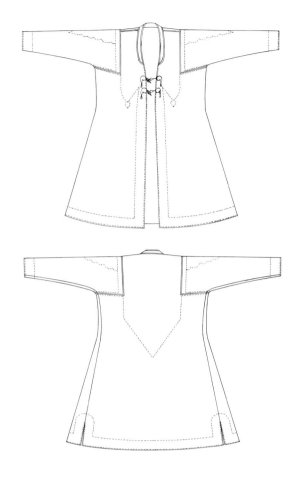

The heavy gold embroidery and couching on this man's woollen robe from northern India is typical of the work done in the Panjab during the nineteenth century. The loose robe itself is originally a Central Asian type, typified by the simple cut and colourful lining with facing in a contrasting colour. Robes like this are not usually worn closed, or are fastened by a sash wrapped around the waist, so these large, decorative gold-thread fastenings would have been mostly for decoration.

Man's robe (*choga*) of wool with gold threadwork.
Northern India (Panjab, acquired in Amritsar in 1855),
mid 19th century
0197 (IS)

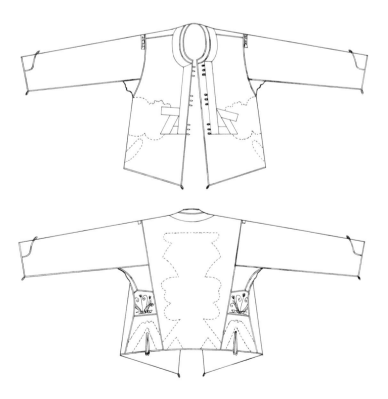

The most obvious decoration on the front of this jacket is the metal braid that encircles the neck, runs down most of the front and then folds back along itself to form Z- and S-shapes. On the right front the braid is placed along the edge but on the left front it is placed 4cm (1¾ inches) in because the jacket fastens right over left. A red silk cord has been applied along both edges and also forms soft loops which are secured under the metal braid on the left front.

Three groups of three buttons have been stitched onto the right front panel. These are made from lead and are surprisingly long. The bulbous half can be seen, the other half forms a thick shaft with a hole at the far end. Because the buttons do not have a short loop holding them in place, they are rigid and because the bulb of the button is right against the edging cord, it is impossible to fix the loop around it.

Man's jacket of felt embroidered
with wool and decorated with metal braid.
Croatia (Obrovac), 19th century
Given by George Hubbard
T.179-1928

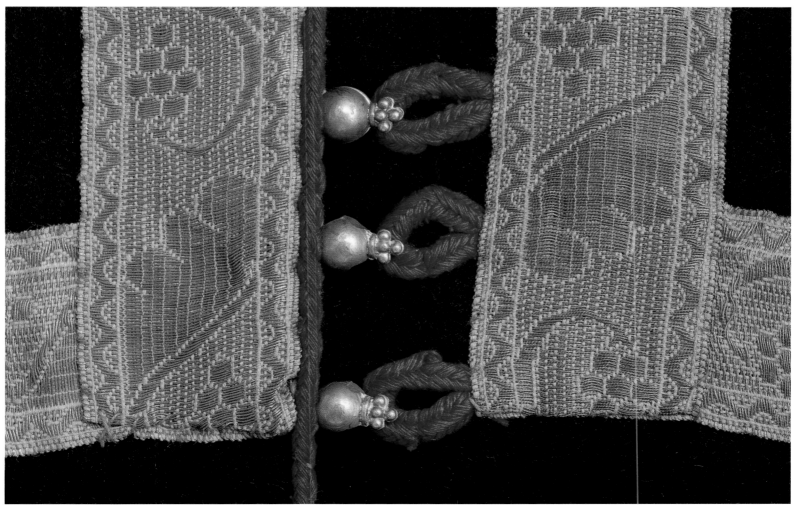

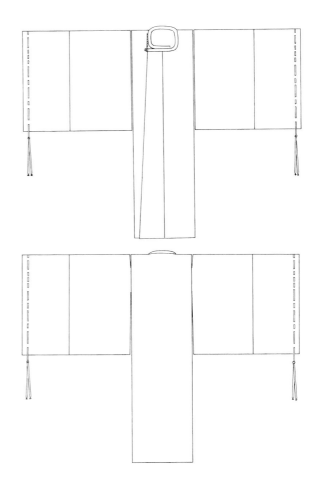

This double-breasted robe with its high, round collar would have been worn by a male member of the Japanese imperial court. The clothing styles of the court were established in the Heian period (794–1185) and changed little over the succeeding centuries. This example dates from the second half of the nineteenth century and is a style of robe known as a *kariginu,* which literally means 'hunting cloth'. It would have been worn as an everyday garment rather than for high ceremony (see also p.76). The sleeves are very wide and secured only at the upper back, while the body is narrow and open at the sides, which would have revealed the garments worn underneath. Layers of thick paper make the neck very stiff and paper wrapped in fabric has been used to create the toggle and loop fastening. Court costumes are traditionally patterned with woven designs. Circular flower motifs, here in bronze on a green ground, are the most common.

Man's court robe (*kariginu*) of woven silk.
Japan, second half of the 19th century
FE.158-1983

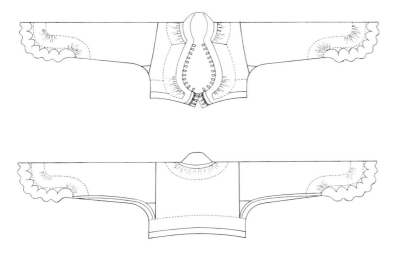

The twenty-four large buttons which edge the low scooped neck of this jacket are purely decorative and it falls to the lot of three small and insignificant ones to fasten it around the wearer's midriff. The method of attaching both the buttons and the loops into which they are secured is unusual: a length of yellow silk cord has been stitched to the left-hand side of the opening so that it forms three large loops with three smaller ones in between. This has been repeated on the right-hand side where a button has been threaded onto each of the three larger loops and stitched in place.

The large decorative buttons are solid (see p.211) but the smaller ones are hollow, enabling them to be threaded onto the yellow cord. Because they are small it is unlikely they have been constructed around a drilled wooden core; instead some woollen or silk fibres will have been formed into a ball around a thin stick or pin which would have been removed once the button was complete.

Woman's short jacket of woven silk decorated
with applied metal braid and cord.
Albania, 19th century
Given by H.C. Game
T.141-1928

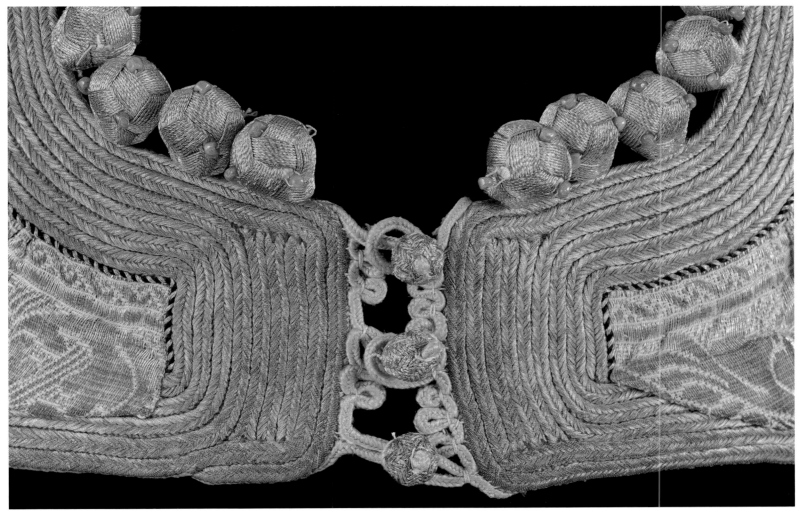

These outsize buttons, four in all, decorate the front of a magenta silk coat from Chinese Turkestan, present-day Xinjiang Region. The gold filigree work set with turquoise and pearls is finished with a coral bead and the entire button is secured through a small loop with twisted wire. The buttons fasten across the chest, leaving the skirt part of the coat open. This facilitates movement, allowing the embroidered garments worn beneath, as well as the coat's bright blue cotton lining, to be seen. The coat forms the top layer of an outfit that was collected between 1928 and 1932 in Khotan (see p.29). The ensemble shows a mix of stylistic elements and materials from China, India and Afghanistan; it can be compared with other garments in the V&A which come from culturally, though not politically, allied regions.

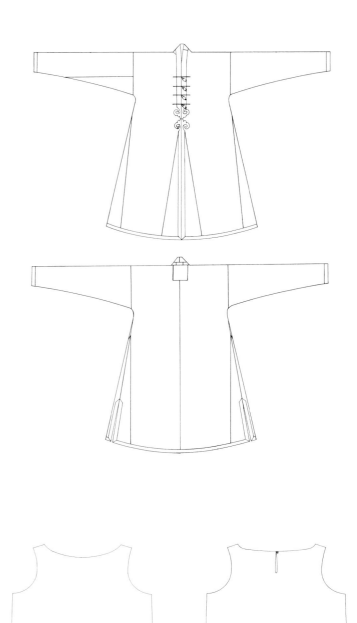

Woman's coat of embroidered silk damask.
China (Xinjiang Autonomous Region),
19th or early 20th century
Given by Captain George Sherriff
T.31-1932

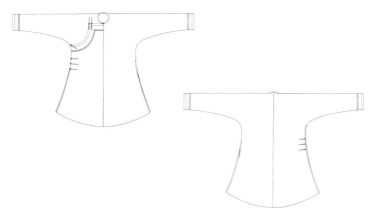

The button fastenings on this woman's long jacket are a variation on the more typical textile knots seen on other Chinese garments. Here, each loop has two buttons, one of which is jade-coloured plastic on a shaft, and the other a stamped metal flowerhead on a ring. They are spaced out along the asymmetric closure, which follows the collarbone before curving down into an arc to close under the arm. The neck and top edge of the overlap section of the jacket are bound with patterned silk gauze. The same silk is used to create the loops for the buttons. The dark brown gauze, with its surface shine, looks particularly handsome against the matt black cotton jacket. This subdued wedding jacket was teamed with a highly decorated skirt similar to that on p.219.

Woman's bridal jacket of cotton and silk.
China (Hoklo people), c.1968
Valery M. Garrett Collection purchased with funds from the
Friends of the V&A
FE.197:1-1995

A loop and knot fastening is used here at the side of a woman's summer top. In this position it serves more as discreet decoration than as a practical fastening although a similar knot and loop secures the garment at the back of the neck. This non-traditional use of a traditional closure is typical of the clothes made by Shanghai Tang, the brainchild of the Hong Kong entrepreneur David Tang. The garment is reversible. It is lined with a silk chiffon, the same weight as the patterned 'outside' but in plain lilac. Exemplifying the Shanghai Tang touch, a plain chiffon fastening is sewn on the patterned side, and a patterned one, just seen in this detail, is sewn on the plain 'inside'. This top is teamed with a matching pair of trousers.

Woman's top of printed silk chiffon.
China (Hong Kong), 1999
Given by David Tang
FE.61:1-1999

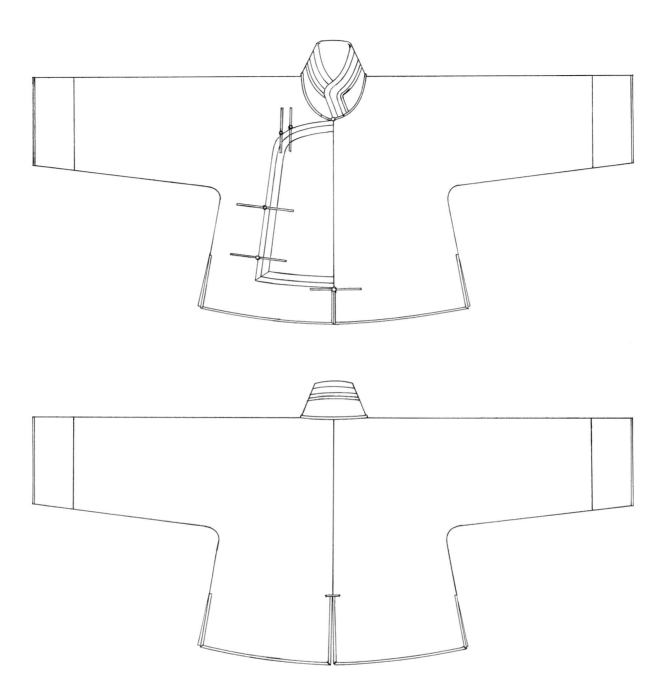

This short jacket derives its impact from the dramatic colouring and bold motifs. The purple ground is embellished with velvet pile in a deeper tone, which is framed by black satin edgings and elongated loops with knot buttons. The crossover section, closing the garment from left to right, is secured by pairing a set of loops and buttons vertically across the collarbone. The other fastenings are arranged horizontally at the neck, at the side, and at the stepped hem respectively. We should not presume that the large design of velvet peonies indicates that this garment was for a woman. It was originally described in the museum records as the type of garment 'worn by Manchurian ladies'. A tag sewn inside the jacket includes the term 'riding jacket', a name commonly used for a Chinese man's short jacket. The Museum acquired this garment from the Japan-British Exhibition held in London in 1910. This event was a showcase for Japanese imperialism, a way of showing that this island nation was bent on widening its spheres of influence. Manchuria, in north-east China, was one of the areas Japan wished to penetrate.

Jacket of silk velvet.
China, 1900–10
Given by the Japanese Imperial Exhibition Commissioners
T.5-1911

This flamboyant fastening is the only visible means of closure on this garment. There are, however, press-studs along the collar-bone, a hook and eye at the neck, and a zip up the right-hand side. This type of dress is known as a *cheongsam* or *qipao* and the decorative frogging became one of its distinctive features. As with most *cheongsam* of this sort, the frogging matches the trim around the edges. Whether they are plain or convoluted, each fastening is composed of two parts. The 'eye' is the half that includes the loop and this part is sewn on the upper side of the dress. The 'head'

incorporates the knot button and is fixed to the lower side. Whereas most *cheongsam* tailors are men, women are employed to make these buttons and loops. Strips of bias-cut cloth are pasted around thin wire, which is then twisted into the desired shape and sewn down onto the dress. The flower formation echoes the flowers woven into the red damask of this garment and there are two 'long life' characters also incorporated into the fastening. The V&A commissioned this dress from the Hong Kong tailor Mr Leung Ching Wah of Linva Tailor.

Woman's dress (*cheongsam* or *qipao*) of red patterned silk.
By Linva Tailor
China (Hong Kong), 1995
FE.313-1995

Cuffs, Edgir
and Sea

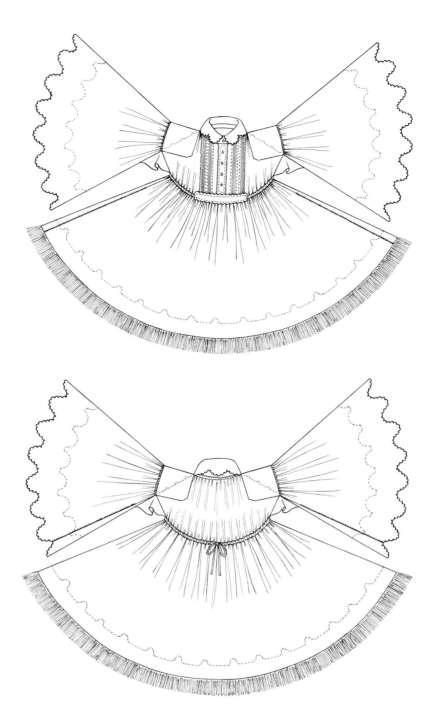

The line drawing for this boy's shirt looks like an angel in flight, a celestial being soaring above the earth. Certainly the enormously wide sleeves would tempt any spirited child to rush around flapping. Each sleeve is decorated with four bands of embroidery: a scalloped edge oversewn with red cotton in buttonhole stitch; a line of circular holes outlined with white cotton in buttonhole stitch; an undulating stem with paired leaves in orange, purple and red cotton and, above these, a deep border of eyelets forming large pear-shaped bushes, which were developed from an Indian motif known as a *boteh*.

Without the eyelets the sheer volume of fabric in each sleeve would have been overwhelming. By oversewing the holes with white cotton and contrasting this with narrow but solid bands of red, the sleeves have become delicate and pretty. A sharp metal die has been used to stamp out the holes and to produce the scalloped edge. It would have been impossible to use scissors or a knife to produce the regularity of this edge, identical diameters for all the holes in the second border and *botehs* of identical size.

Boy's shirt of cotton embroidered with cotton.
Hungary (Mezőkövesd), second half of the 19th century
73-1903

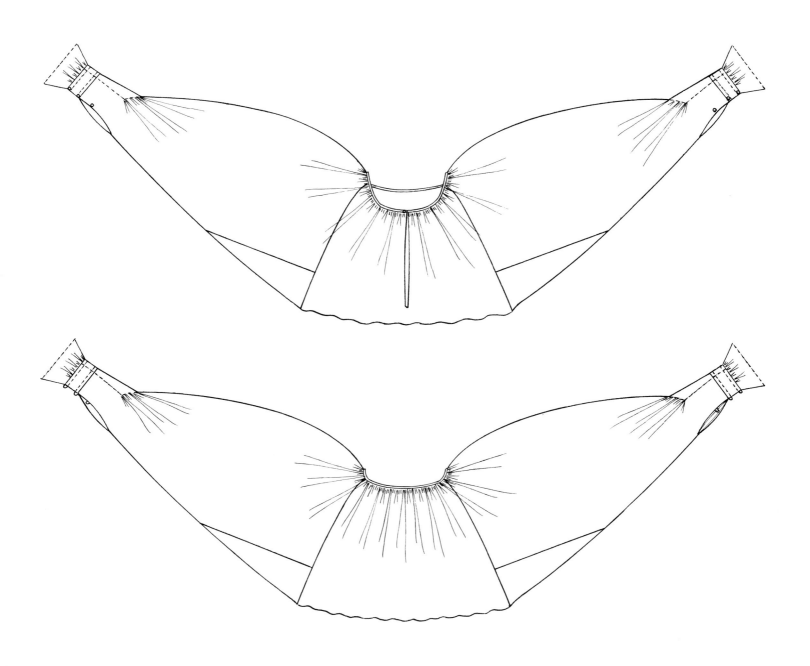

The wide sleeves of this blouse have been drawn into a long and narrow cuff that tapers towards the wrist and then flares out over the hand, ending with a flourish of lace. Everything appears to be white and because there are no bright, gaudy colours to distract the eye, the skill demonstrated here lies in combining different textures to create a pleasing effect, which is both subtle and elegant.

There are three parts to the cuff: in the upper part, much of which would have been obscured as the full sleeve billowed over it, excess fabric has been gathered and secured by smocking with cream silk thread. The smocking has been continued in a central cylinder of fabric attached to the rest of the cuff, above and below, by a tube of cotton which has been folded back upon itself and stitched to form a zigzag. The lower part of the cuff has been tightly gathered along the top and then falls free and has been trimmed with an applied edging of bobbin lace.

The cuff fastens with three small buttons. There is no decoration elsewhere on the blouse because it would have been worn beneath an outer garment – probably beneath a *sarafan* (see p.44).

Woman's blouse of figured cotton embroidered
with silk and edged with cotton bobbin lace.
Russia, 19th century
499-1907

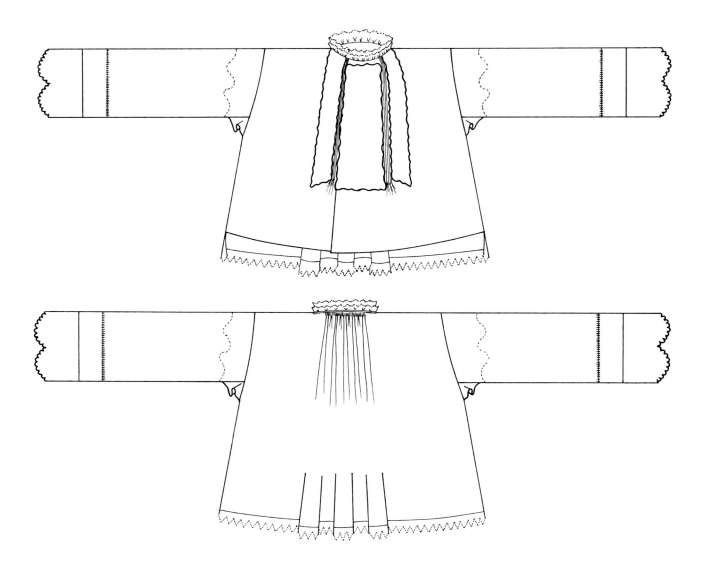

Brightly coloured, solid, shiny embroidery almost entirely covers the straight sleeves on this blouse. There is no finesse in the design, no great skill demonstrated by the embroiderer but there is obvious delight in the abundance of colour and in the scale and profusion of the blossoms. The silk is barely twisted, its fibres lying almost parallel like floss silk, and so it forms a very reflective surface. No great care has been taken with the large satin stitch embroidery and coloured threads are carried loosely across the back of the work from one motif to another. The speed with which the work might have been finished seems to have been the foremost consideration.

Yellow silk has been used to attach the sleeve to the separate cuff which has been embroidered in a similar manner. Yellow is picked up again as a highlight in the deep border of machine-embroidery that forms the final section. The large eyelets and the scalloped edge create the general impression of lace so that the decoration of the sleeve changes in intensity from the upper block of massed flowers, through a more delicate floral border to finish with a line of holes edged with silk.

Woman's blouse of cotton embroidered
with silk and edged with applied machine-embroidery.
Croatia (Sisak), late 19th or early 20th century
Given by Mr and Mrs C.O. Wakefield-Harvey
T.29A-1958

The tablet-woven braid that runs diagonally from the upper left towards the lower right of this sleeve is quite astonishing. It is made from many colours of silk thread forming fine stripes and its lower part has been embroidered with metal thread across the width to form more complex patterns. The diagonal opening it decorates is on the under part of the wrist and would not always have been obvious, but attention to detail was evidently important.

A corner of the lower sleeve is seen here: it has been lined with green silk velvet and edged with a woven metal braid. Metal threads decorate the rest of the jacket but they appear unremarkable compared with the exquisite beauty of the short length of embroidered braid on each cuff.

Man's jacket, silk velvet embroidered with metal thread and trimmed with metal cord and silk braid.
Albanian, c.1810
Given by Jane Blakemore
T.1114-2000

The intricate basket patterns in the gold-wrapped thread on this sleeve are ingeniously formed by the arrangement of the orange silk thread used to couch it down, as well as the disposition of the metallic thread itself. A thick cord of the same gold-wrapped thread and orange silk is used to define the edge of the cuff and strengthen it. This Baluch dress is unusual not in the intricacy of its embroidery but in the lavishness of its materials. Dresses of this type (see pp.112, 154) rarely use metallic thread in their decoration, and are much more frequently decorated with coloured silks.

Woman's dress (pashk) of silk with couched gold-wrapped thread.
Pakistan (Baluchistan, probably from Kalat), early 20th century
IM.65-1930

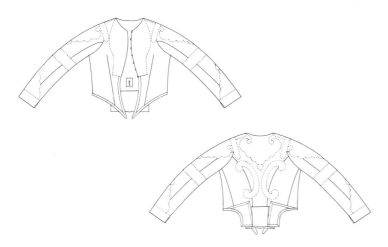

This unusual jacket is based on European military styles, although obviously intended for quite a small Nepalese boy. The materials used are also far from the usual military conventions, combining European patterned velvets with elaborate cuffs and front panels heavily embroidered with seed pearls, sequins and gold-wrapped thread. Western dress uniforms contributed a great deal to formal wear in northern India and Nepal during the later nineteenth century, with many hybrid garments coming into vogue at the Indian and Nepalese courts. This little jacket is an example of just such a garment, looking more like a piece of theatrical costume than something worn by a young courtier in Kathmandu in the 1850s.

Boy's velvet jacket with gold embroidery and seed pearls.
Nepal (Kathmandu), acquired in 1855
038 (IS)

The sleeves of this robe are only seamed from the underarm to the elbow from where they would hang, dangling to reveal the lining of blue silk, embroidered with floral sprays and pink sequins.

Despite the large amounts of metal thread used to decorate the wool, most of the glitter comes from applied sequins. The metal strip was not closely wound around its yellow silk core and much of it has come away. The rows of metal braid, cords and fancy edgings are decorative but also add weight to the end of the sleeve ensuring that it hangs well.

A thin layer of woollen fibres has been used throughout the garment as padding between the embroidered wool and its lining; lines of running stitch, keeping the padding in place, can be seen on the lining.

Woman's robe (entari) of wool twill padded with woollen fibres and embroidered with silk and metal thread.
Turkey (Kütahya), second half of the 19th century
Given by Mrs M.H. Rolland
T.30-1943

The weight of heavy, gold embroidered edgings attached to fine cotton or silk ground fabrics has often meant that fragile courtly garments like this woman's shirt had a short life and were then discarded. It was common practice in the Indian subcontinent, however, to recycle costly and elaborate edgings on another garment, thereby prolonging their useful lives. The embroidered edgings on this shirt cuff, which is also used around the neck and hem, includes silver-gilt domed sequins, ribbons of metal-wrapped thread and strips of beaten gilt silver. The pristine condition of this shirt suggests that it was never (or very rarely) worn, and it has been preserved in the collections of the Indian Museum and then the V&A since 1855. The neckline is illustrated on p. 27.

Woman's shirt (*kurta*) of cotton, with silk and metal embroidery.
Pakistan (Lahore), *c.*1855
6157 (IS)

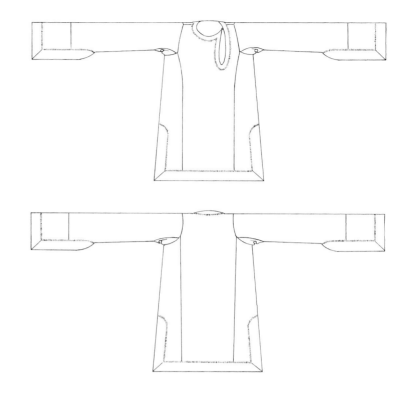

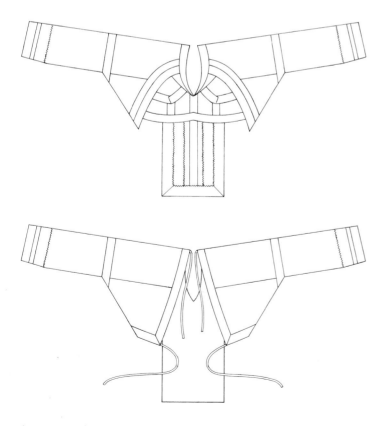

Applied ribbon of *gota*, made of thin strips of flattened gold wire woven together with silk or cotton thread, is traditionally a very popular form of decoration in northern India. On this bodice, it has been applied as flat strips, in zigzag patterns and as cut-out leaf forms, with additional bands of tightly folded *gota* adding emphasis to the front panel and the edge of the cuffs, shown here. This type of green silk ground fabric was particularly popular in Panjab and northern Rajasthan in the nineteenth century. This blouse would be worn with a full skirt and a large head-cover to cover the head and upper body.

Woman's blouse (*choli*) of red and green silk with applied metal ribbon (*gota*).
India (Panjab), 1867
05465 (IS)

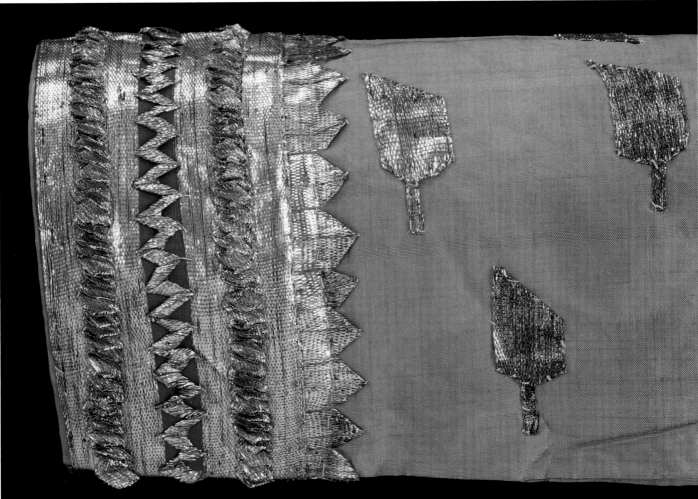

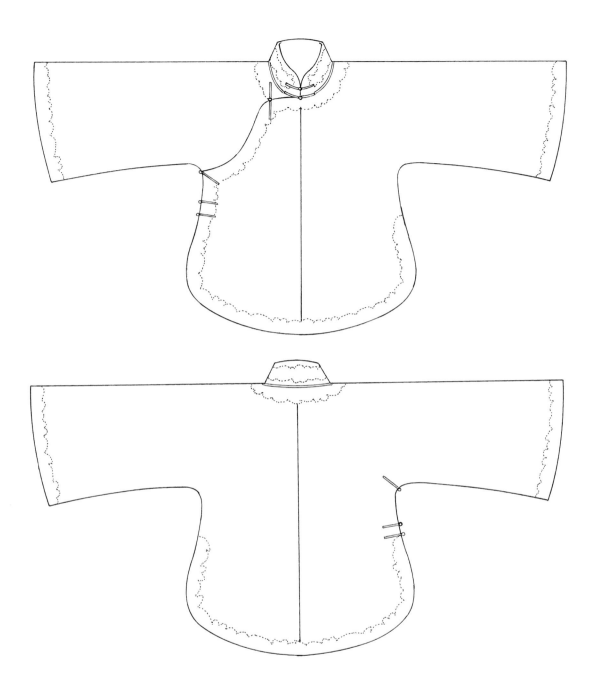

The fashion for this kind of cuff came in around 1900. The style represents a departure from both the straight sleeve end and the horse-hoof cuff seen on Chinese clothes elsewhere in this book. This particular jacket dates from 1915 when the donor was a young woman living in Shanghai. Although Mrs Roney used this jacket herself, there is little to distinguish it from those worn by Chinese women at the same period. The bright green silk, patterned with a design that must have seemed modern at the time, is set off by the machine-made openwork edging in shades of black, beige and white. This was probably manufactured in Switzerland and imported into China. The Chinese tailor may have had it in stock or his customer could have purchased it herself and asked him to incorporate it into the design. The edging goes around each cuff and also round the neck, side fastening and hem. The shape of the hem, a more pronounced curve than the sleeve ends, is also a new feature of the early twentieth century. The lining, not visible in this detail but seen at the cuff edge, is an antidote to the green being made of ivory floral damask. This type of jacket was generally teamed with a black silk skirt.

Woman's jacket of woven silk.
China, c.1915
Given by Mrs M.B. Roney
FE.64-1997

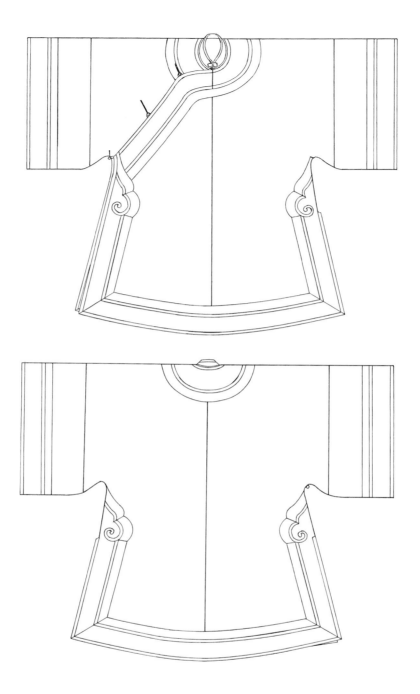

This wide sleeve, here seen from the back, is gracefully shaped where it joins the body of the robe. The cuff end is decorated with an applied band of embroidery. The style of these sleevebands varies, but they always provide a contrast to the garment either in colour, technique or motifs. Here, although the disparity is evident, white floss silk is used for some of the embroidery adorning the cuffs and for the flowers on the main body of the robe, which gives a visual unity to the garment. This sleeveband, in mid-blue satin, is also embroidered with multicoloured vignettes of animals and birds in seed stitch, a type of knot stitch that adds some depth. The embroidered bands attached to the right and left cuffs do not match each other, the coloured creatures being different on each side. Sleevebands were created in the domestic sphere as well as in professional workshops. We have no evidence to suggest whether bands were designed for particular robes or whether a ready-made band was chosen to suit the garment. On this robe, in addition to the embroidered band, there are three narrow warp-patterned ribbons and a black satin bias edging.

Woman's robe of embroidered black silk.
China, 19th century
Given by Mr F. Twyman
T.26-1958

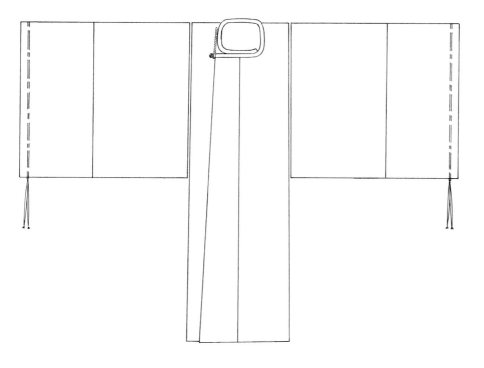

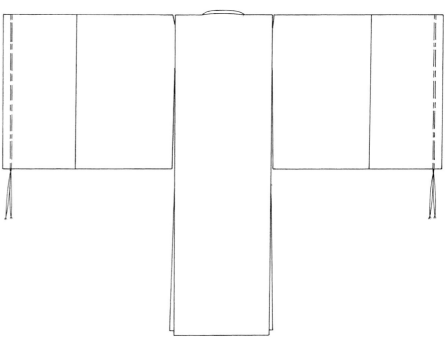

Japanese robes are differentiated by their style of sleeve. Those with small openings at the wrist are known as *kōsode* (see p.136), while robes such as this, with a wide wrist opening that extends along the entire width of the sleeve, are called *ōsode*. This kind of large, loose sleeve allows for a layered look as the edges of the garments worn underneath are revealed at the sleeve opening of the upper garment. Voluminous *ōsode*, made of stiff, woven fabrics, are worn at the imperial court. This garment is a *kariginu* or 'hunting cloth' (see p.52). To allow for maximum ease of movement when drawing a bow on horseback, the double width sleeves are attached to the body of the garment only at the upper back and the cords threaded along the cuffs allow the sleeve to be gathered up. This example was made in the second half of the nineteenth century, by which time *kariginu* were no longer worn for hunting, but as part of the everyday costume of court nobles. It is a summer garment, the open structure of the gauze making it perfect for hot, humid weather. Worn over other robes, the transparency of the cloth would have created a shimmering effect.

Man's court robe (*kariginu*) of silk gauze.
Japan, second half of the 19th century
FE.157-1983

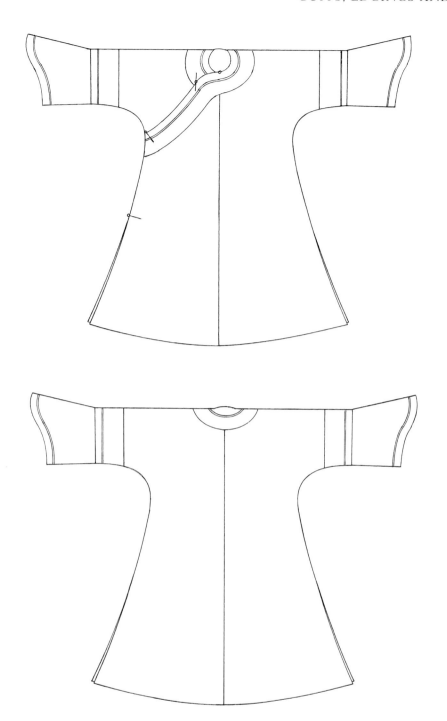

This type of embroidered and edged cuff was worn by people of Manchu origin. They introduced it to China when they took power there in the seventeenth century. The Chinese term for this shape of cuff is translated as 'horse-hoof', an appropriate name because both Manchu men and women were skilled horse riders. There is no suggestion that this particular garment was worn for riding even though the cut of the cuff might well be convenient for holding reins and protecting the hands at the same time. The cuff is in contrasting material to the rest of the garment, a common dressmaking feature of ladies' robes from this part of the world for some centuries. There are two bands of coloured silk embroidery on black satin and, although both bands have the same design of flowers and butterflies, each is on a slighter different scale. They are edged in a braid of gold-wrapped thread and a strip of woven gold silk. The rest of the gown, which may date from the eighteenth century, is quite different, being made from a soft yellow satin embroidered in a limited palette of pale blues and white. It has a floral theme, like the cuffs, and a vertically striped hem of the kind seen throughout the eighteenth and nineteenth centuries on both men's and women's clothes.

Woman's robe of embroidered silk.
China (Manchu), 18th and 19th centuries
Bequeathed by Dame Ada Macnaghten
T.52-1970

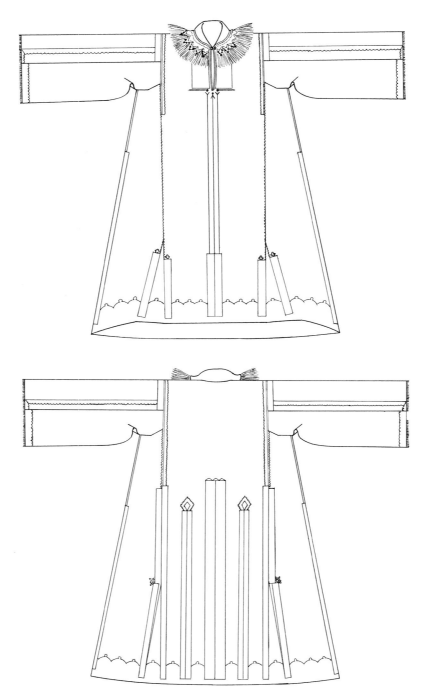

The straight sleeve of this dress is made from two types of cotton cloth: the panel which forms the under part is plainweave while the upper was woven with a pattern of small diamonds and then almost entirely covered with embroidery. The use of two different fabrics suggests that the embroidered panel was either re-used from an older, worn-out dress (which was a common practice) or that it had been purchased. When the sleeve is worn extended to its full length the lower edge is trimmed with just a bright red strip of plush. When it is turned to form a cuff, however, another world is revealed.

The lower part of each sleeve has been faced with a band of cotton velvet richly embroidered with wool and trimmed with a metal braid, pink glass beads and pink sequins. Large white stitches hold the facing in place and can be seen between the braid and the red fringe. These decorations were mass-produced in large urban centres and followed the prevailing fashions. When they are found on the traditional dress of peasant communities, it is usually in small quantities because of their relative expense. The wearer of this dress did not have enough embroidered velvet to make complete facings and there is a 3.5cm (1½ inches) gap on the inside of each sleeve.

Woman's dress of cotton embroidered with wool.
Macedonia (Skopska Črnagora near Skopje), 19th century
Given by Mrs Lucy Duke Kinne
T.264-1990

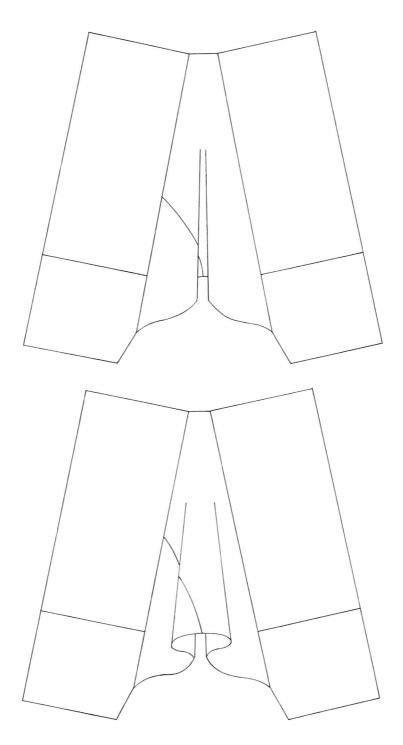

These elegant trousers were collected in Singapore in 1855. They are made up of two of the most elaborate types of cloth woven in the Malay Peninsula – silk patterned with weft ikat and silk with supplementary weft decoration of gold-wrapped thread (*songket*). The *songket* panels are attached to the lower edge of the trousers at approximately knee level, probably to give additional strength to the garment as well as to show off this costly fabric. Although the flamboyant decoration on these trousers may suggest that they were intended for a woman, it was only in certain areas of Muslim South-East Asia that women wore trousers rather than the traditional tubular skirt, and the Malay Peninsula was not one of them. The ikat-patterned fabric here shows the influence of Indian trade cloths, especially the double-ikat *patola,* on local South-East Asian textile design.

Man's trousers of silk with weft-ikat
and gold-wrapped thread decoration (*songket*).
Malaysia (probably Trengganu), mid 19th century
5645 (IS)

These trousers are made of fine striped silk fabric, and are cut loose around the waist and thighs, but taper to a close-fitting lower section that is typical of the Indian subcontinent. This narrow section would often be wrinkled up to the knee in a style called *churidar,* which means 'with bangles'. In more recent times, this narrow leg section would be bias-cut to give a more clinging effect, but surviving nineteenth-century trousers all seem to have straight-cut legs. On this pair, the decorative effect is concentrated on the simple but elegant embroidered cuff. The trousers would be worn with a long, straight shirt, probably also with embroidered decoration.

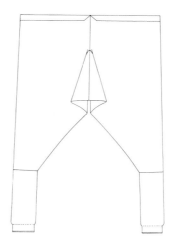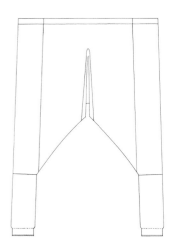

Woman's trousers of silk with embroidered cuffs.
Pakistan (probably Sindh), mid 19th century
6047 (IS)

This detail shows the long edge of a sari, perhaps the best known item of dress from Asia. Many women who live in the Indian subcontinent, or who have their roots there, continue to wear this draped garment and it is subject to frequent fashion changes and regional variations. This sari is an example of cross-cultural interchange. It was made in China for the Parsi community, today a much-dispersed group of people originating in present-day Iran. They settled first in Gujarat where they retained their distinctive culture and set of beliefs although Parsi women adopted the sari there. The black ground of this piece, together with the use of Chinese embroidery, are elements that distinguish it specifically as a Parsi sari. Silk gauze, as here, was a favoured material and purple, as well as black, was a commonly occurring colour. In many cases, the edging on these Parsi pieces is applied separately, yards of satin ribbon being embroidered by Chinese artisans for this express purpose. Here, however, the edging is embroidered straight onto the sari silk.

Woman's sari of embroidered silk.
China (Indian Parsi community), first half of the 20th century
Given by Sir Harold E. Satow
T.24-1967

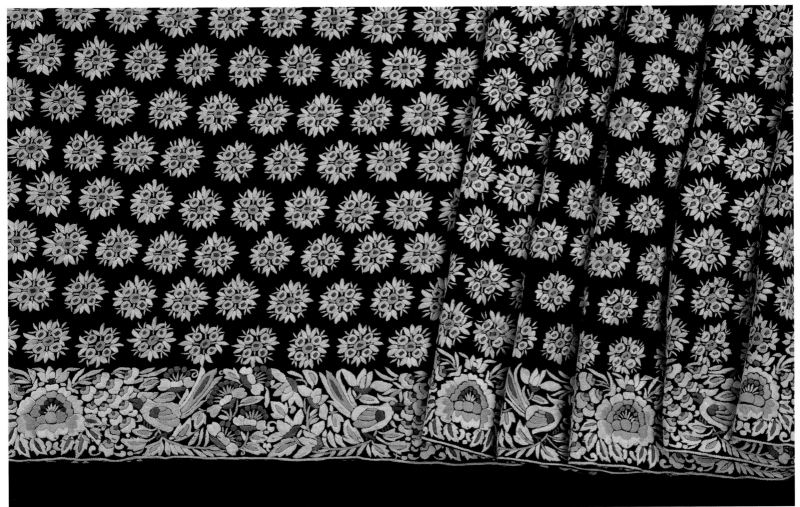

The side seams of this robe barely extend below the hips and from that point downwards the back and the front panels are separate, opening to reveal the trousers which would have been worn underneath, and to show their own lining of blue silk damask. An imported European furnishing fabric has been used. The ground of the damask is moiré – an effect produced by using heavy rollers to impress a watered pattern on the ribbed ground.

The silk used for the robe was woven with a fine stripe at wide intervals and a meandering floral stem has been embroidered in the intervening spaces. This pattern was first printed with dark ink, which can be seen clearly in many places, and was then embroidered using a tambour hook. Tambour work is only possible if the fabric is held very tightly in a frame. It takes its name from the French word for a drum because many early tambour frames were drum-shaped; it is a quick method of covering the ground with a fine chain stitch. The completed length of woven and embroidered silk was then cut into appropriate pieces for the robe. It has been edged with a loose metal braid.

Woman's robe (*entari*) of striped silk embroidered with silk.
Turkey, 19th century
Given by Mr and Mrs John Makower
T.197-1964

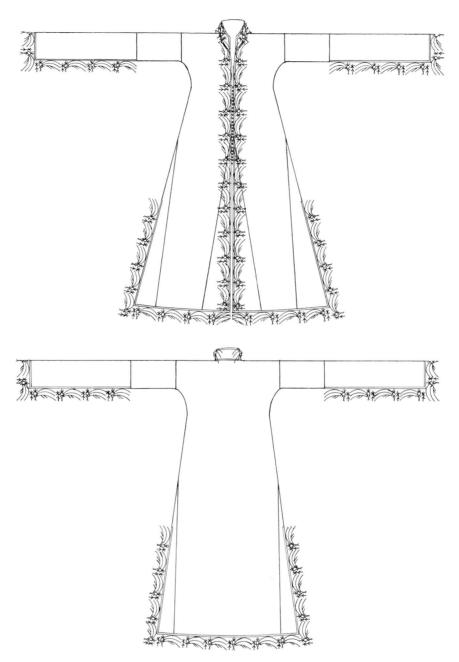

This is a gown to be seen in and to be admired. It is said to have been worn by a bride as part of a wedding ceremony but it is not designed for movement and not necessarily for close inspection.

It is made from a length of green silk on which a floral pattern was printed or drawn and then embroidered with couched metal thread and lines of glittering sequins. The silk was cut into the pieces required for the robe – cutting and seaming through the embroidery. In an age and culture where hand-decoration is expensive, this seems like sacrilege but it is not an uncommon practice where labour is relatively cheap. The edges have been decorated with an elaborate trimming of metal thread, which has been twisted and stitched into a complex floral motif. There is no backing and so the trimming is floppy and as it inevitably falls to one side it reveals the unsightly tacking stitches that hold the individual metal threads in place. But this is a presentation gown, in which the wearer was expected to stand perfectly still. This style of garment is designed to trail on the floor, with each panel elegantly arranged over and around her feet. Immobilized in this way, each part of the trimming could be carefully adjusted to create a breathtaking vision of green and gold.

Woman's gown (*entari*) of silk embroidered with metal thread and sequins.
Turkey, *c*.1900
Given by Miss Inés de Vaudry. This gown belonged to her mother,
Princess Eff-keen-Oskanyan, a member of the Armenian Christian
community in Istanbul.
T.96-1954

Despite being covered with tightly packed flowers worked in couched metal thread, the silk pile of this purple velvet coat has almost completely disappeared. This is unlikely to have been caused by wear and tear – the raised embroidery would have protected it – but the silk may have been treated with a substance that accidentally accelerated the natural process of decay.

The repeating pattern of gold flowerheads linked by short stems is rather subdued but it provides a solid pattern to contrast with the dramatic swirling silver cords which form the edging. In fact the metal thread used to create the flowers is not gold, nor even gilt; it is silver strip wound around a yellow silk core with several strands twisted together to form a cord.

The applied woven braid is also silver but appears to have a golden sheen when it is placed next to the pure silver colour of the edging. This has been made by stitching silver thread in a chevron pattern onto dark red silk cords. The cords were coiled into fluid swirls, secured by stitches on the reverse and then attached to the edge of the coat. A small square of woven braid has been inserted from the back to fill in gaps formed by the wave-like undulations which themselves have been edged with a row of tightly coiled silver cords.

Woman's sleeveless coat of silk velvet embroidered
with metal thread and applied braid and cord.
Serbia, second half of the 19th century
895-1902

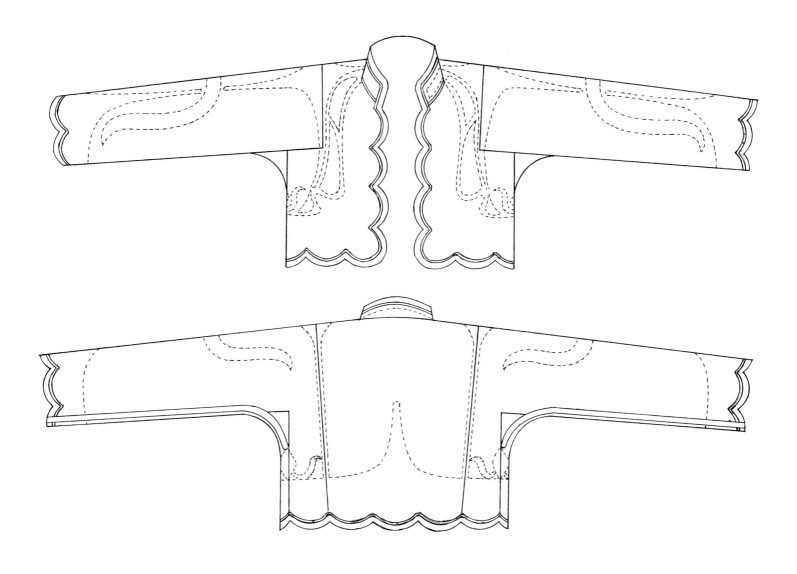

Adding embroidery to silk velvet, which is one of the most sumptuous fabrics, is like gilding a lily – it seems unnecessary, but few can deny that the results are astonishing. This red velvet jacket has been smothered with gold thread, laid on the surface in intricate interlacings and secured to the velvet by minute, almost invisible silk stitches. The use of the couching technique ensured that no expensive metal thread was wasted by being taken through to the reverse side.

A short line of yellow tacking stitches can be seen a little way in from the right hand edge of the image. These were used as a first step to mark out the main areas of the pattern and were often left in place when the embroidery was finished. Pins would have been used to secure small areas of metal threads in their convoluted swirls until they could be couched in place. Because velvet is a pile fabric it is difficult to mark a pattern onto it for the embroiderer to follow. At best only the general outlines could be given, so although the pattern on the two front panels is very similar, they are not identical.

Woman's jacket of silk velvet embroidered with metal thread.
South-eastern Europe (probably Athens, Greece),
mid 19th century
T.773-1919

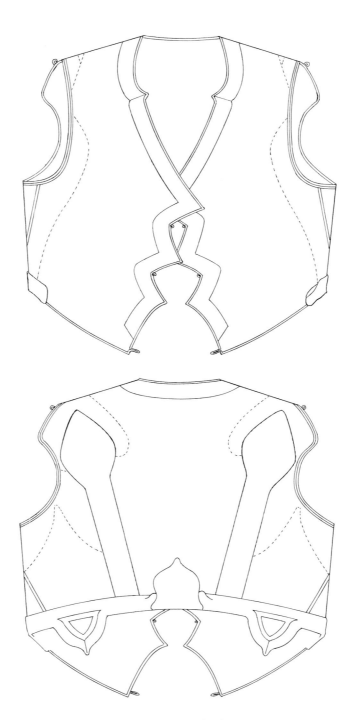

There is a lot of movement in the shape and decoration of this waistcoat, every cutting line and every line of decoration is curved. It fastens with a single hook and eye at the bottom of the V-shaped neck and then both front panels fall away on the diagonal across what must have been the strong barrel-chest of the man for whom it was made. The white felted wool has been cut to form three points down the front and several rows of black silk cord have been attached to the edge and twisted to follow the contours. When the waistcoat was made, the edges were faced with woollen braid which survives beneath a later white silk lining, part of which can be seen beyond the cord edging.

The thick silk cords used to decorate the front panels have a pronounced twist, giving it a rope-like quality but despite this it forms flowers and leaves of surprising liveliness. Enough of the white ground shows to provide a contrast to the sombre black silk and the curving lines, which enclose a meandering stem of leaves, prevent the tightly packed flowerheads from becoming monotonous.

Man's waistcoat of felted wool embroidered with silk cord.
Montenegro, 19th century
Given by George Hubbard
T.182-1928

This crisply embroidered woman's jacket is cut in typical Burmese fashion, with projecting side flaps over the hips and a rectangular panel behind the front opening. The quilted cotton embroidered with yellow silk suggests the influence of eastern Indian embroideries, and may indeed have been done by Indian embroiderers in Burma. Some elements of the pattern, like the 'twisted rope' design, are more recognizably Burmese and recur on the multi-coloured Burmese woven silks called *acheik* or *luntaya*. These patterns are used to follow the outlines of the edges of the jacket, giving more emphasis to the angularity of the garment's corners.

Woman's jacket of cotton embroidered with silk.
Myanmar (Burma), mid 19th century
5631 (IS)

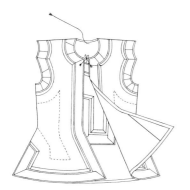

Elaborate velvet and gold-encrusted jackets and coats were very popular as court wear in nineteenth-century Burma. This flamboyant jacket, made for a military official of the court at Mandalay, combines elements of European and Indian dress with a traditional Burmese cut, with its projecting side-panels and separate front panel (like the other Burmese garment on this page). The embroidery, in which silver-gilt sequins are formed into rosettes, is very reminiscent of Indian *zardozi* work, and was probably done by professional Indian embroiderers, either in India or Burma itself. This jacket was teamed with a long, sleeved robe of deep red velvet (also in the V&A collection) and a spectacular 'cloud-collar' with points that stand up from the shoulder.

Man's jacket of velvet with woven gold edging and sequins.
Myanmar (Burma), (Mandalay), *c.*1880
Given by Mr H.D. Colt
IS.256a-1960

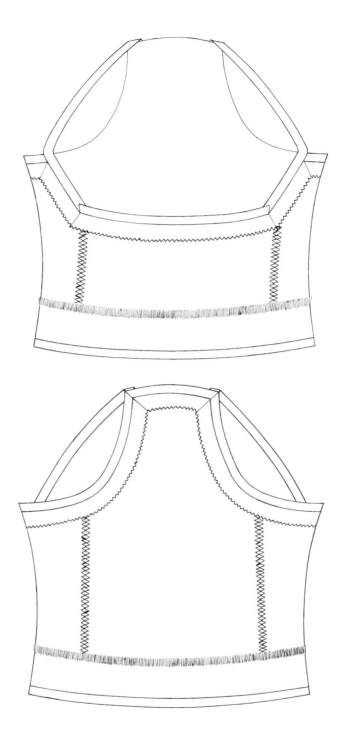

The edges of this diaphanous blouse are decorated with a lavish edging strip of crimped gold ribbon (*gota*), a fringe of alternating gold and silver tinsel and tiny beads sewn onto silk strips in floral and leaf patterns. The elaborate embroidery of this edging is particularly remarkable in comparison with the incredibly delicate green silk ground fabric, which has perished in many places, partly because of the weight of the embroidered borders. This style of bodice, with a halter neck, is called an *angia*, and this example was acquired as part of the so-called 'Queen of Oudh's costume'. This was actually more likely to have been worn by a young dancer than a noblewoman of Avadh, known to the British as Oudh. It was worn with a long, diaphanous over-shirt, a large veil covering the head and upper body and wide-legged trousers.

Woman's bodice of silk with gold thread and bead edging.
Northern India (probably Lucknow), mid 19th century
5838 (IS)

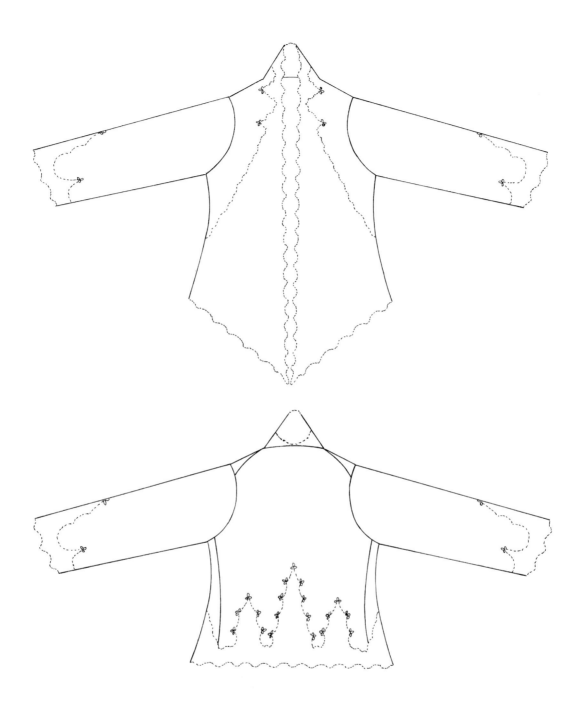

Tailored jackets for both men and women were introduced into the islands of South-East Asia with the spread of Islam, although the shape of this twentieth-century *kebaya* also shows some Western influence in its waisted shape and decorative edging. Jackets like this are traditionally worn particularly by Javanese and Malay women. Lace was a favourite edging material, but here this has been emulated in an elaborate cut-out and embroidered openwork design which is perfect for the airy coolness of tropical dress. The *kebaya* is often worn over a simple breast-cloth and is traditionally fastened with a set of three decorative brooches down the front, which draw the two edges together, with the long front panels hanging down over a wrapped sarong.

Woman's jacket (*kebaya*) of cotton with cut work and silk embroidery.
Indonesia (Java), early 20th century
Given by Jonathan Hope
IS.122-1983

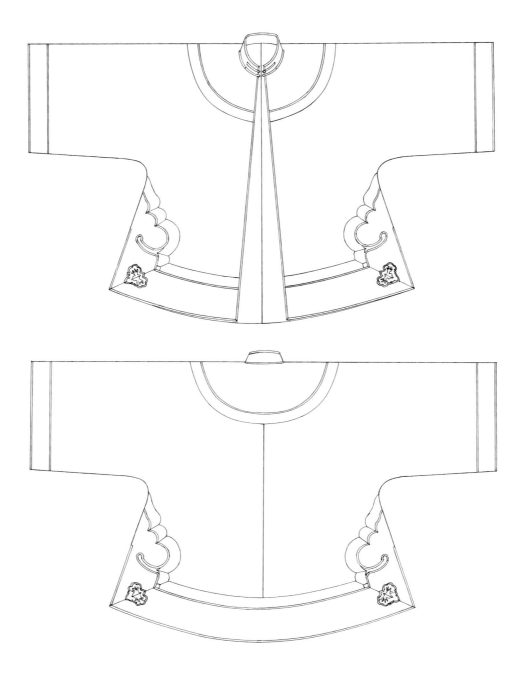

This detail is a carefully executed example of cutwork, a technique used in China in the early years of the twentieth century. It appears at the corner of the jacket hem. It is composed of a cutaway section, and a filled-in section, both in the form of a butterfly, sewn down onto a pale mauve silk insertion beneath. The edges are neatened with black piping. This butterfly decoration, repeated on the opposite side and on the back as well, slants across the corner. The other fancy edgings have been applied so as to reinforce this diagonal feel and together they create interesting shapes and spaces. The detail, while decorative, adds some weight to the garment's edge, preventing the jacket from riding up when worn. This jacket is part of a suit. It is teamed with matching trousers, both garments being made from purple silk sprigged with white blossoms and edged in a bright blue satin. Matching suits like this one are a phenomenon of the late nineteenth and early twentieth centuries and were designed for young women. After marriage, women tended to wear a wraparound skirt over the top of the trousers.

Girl's jacket of resist-dyed silk.
China, early 20th century
T.124-1961

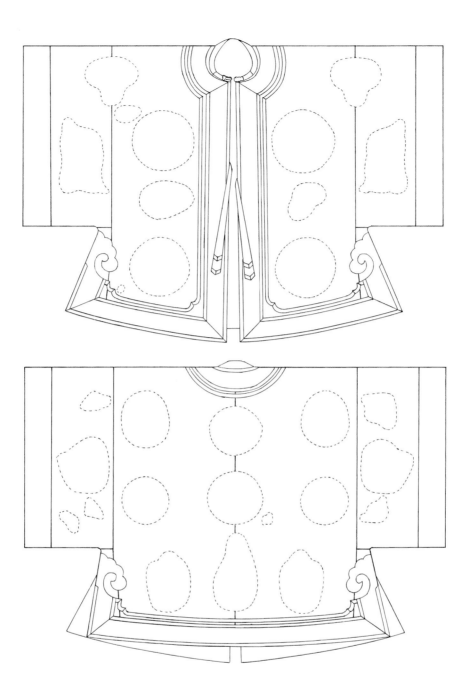

This detail exemplifies the meticulous attention that skilled Chinese artisans paid to the borders of garments. The entire robe is framed with several different trims, which cohere visually because they are confined to shades of blue, black and white. The part of the garment pictured is the trimming for the side slit, always the site of the densest decoration on Chinese women's clothing of this type. It accentuated the sway of the hips as the wearer walked along, often on bound feet. The wide band, densely covered with blue embroidery, goes along the hem, turns the corner with a neat mitre, and then blossoms out into a curlicue shape just above the side-slit

opening. The curl is stretched over, and stuck down onto, a cotton base cut to shape and covered with paste. The paste also helps to bond the underside of this now stiffened scroll to the ground material and it is sewn down as well. This band is sandwiched between narrow bias-cut satin lengths in blue and slightly wider ones in black. The tiny blue edgings are folded and tucked under the wider bands and manipulated skillfully so that the blue always retains an even width throughout. A similar, though narrower, embroidered band is applied inside the broad band and is itself flanked in blue.

Woman's robe of embroidered silk.
China, 19th century
Bequeathed by Mrs S.G. Bishop
T.2-1957

This distinctively cut jacket is worn as Nepalese court or official wear, paired with trousers of the same material. A similar form also occurs with sleeves. This jacket is made of an unusual glazed cotton fabric, quilted all over and with a larger, geometric quilted pattern forming a border. The origin of this style of garment is unclear, but is probably to be found in northern India. Coats and jackets with side fastenings are widespread in both India and Tibet, Nepal's closest neighbours. However, a Tibetan garment would normally use a button- and loop-fastening as a closure, while fabric ties like those on this garment are the more common means of fastening in India.

Man's jacket (*labeda*) of glazed and quilted cotton.
Nepal, early 20th century
Given by Mr G. Haythornthwaite
IS.79-1988

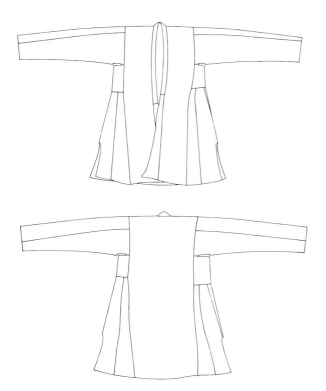

This coat is made of thick woollen cloth woven in the far north-west of Pakistan, where the severe winters and high altitude make warm clothing essential. The decoration on this garment is a simple embroidered pattern of circles and crosses, but more elaborate designs on hats and coats from the same area point to a close relationship with similar garments from the neighbouring Central Asian republic of Tajikistan. The Central Asian connection is also reinforced by the cut of the coat, which is basically that of the open-fronted *choga* (see p.50 for another example). This coat, however, only has a very simple border decoration, in contrast to the colourful contrasting linings and borders often seen on more elaborate, urban *chogas*.

Coat of wool with embroidery.
Pakistan (probably from the Upper Chitral Valley, North-West Frontier Province), 20th century
IS.37-1996

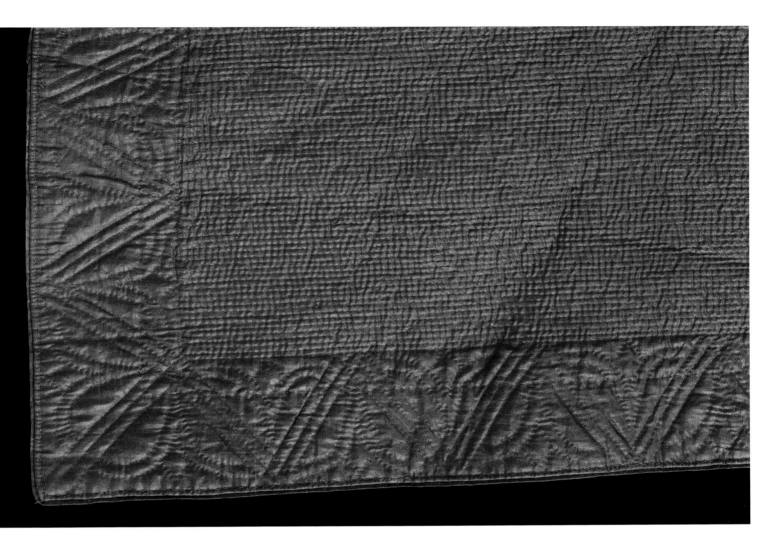

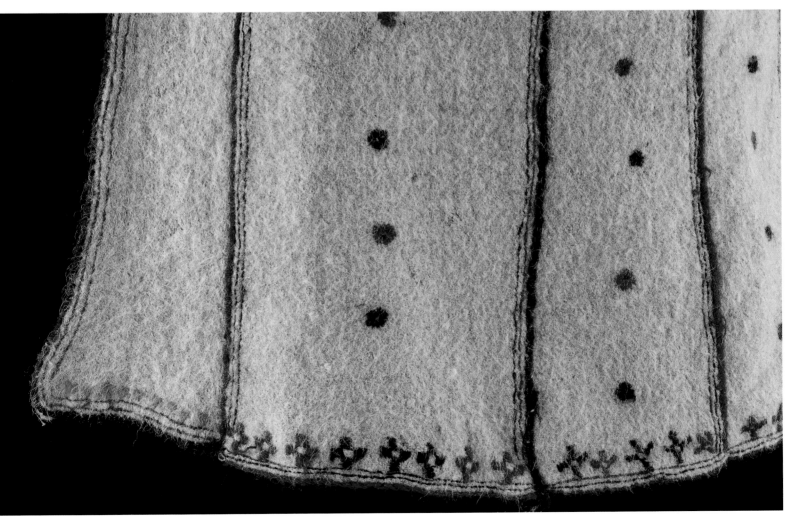

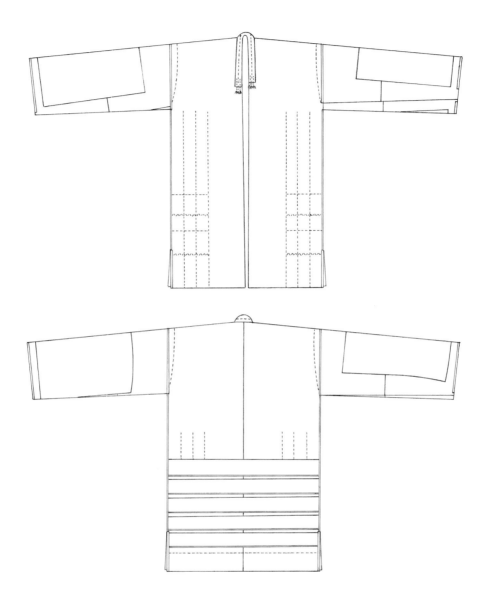

It is perhaps surprising that the beautifully embroidered panels on this woman's jacket are on the lower half of the back of the garment, rather than in a prominent position on the front, which is very sparsely decorated. The colourful edging to the side seams (shown in this detail) also alleviates the plainness of the main part of the garment. The women of the Akha tribe of northern Thailand would wear it with a gathered skirt, leggings decorated with appliqué strips, a simple under-blouse and an elaborate head-dress covered with silver ornaments and beads. This splendid ensemble would be worn every day, not just on special occasions.

Woman's jacket of cotton, embroidered with silk.
Northern Thailand (Akha tribe), 20th century
IS. 75-1990

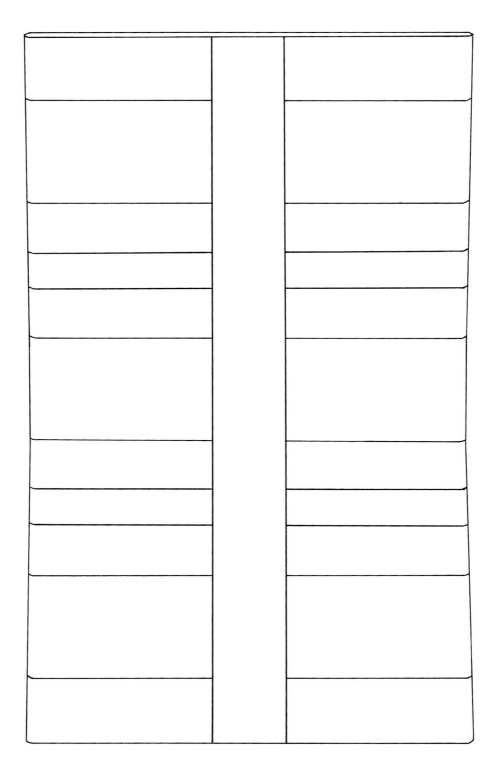

Tubular skirts and dresses are worn in many parts of Asia and else-where in the world. This one is from the Philippines, and is worn by women of the Maranao people of Mindanao, the southernmost island of the Philippines. The brilliant magenta and yellow bands, once the sole prerogative of royalty, are typical of the region, as are the tapestry-woven strips that join the pieces together horizontally and close the vertical seam. This technique, although woven by Muslim weavers in this case, appears to be a product of trade with China, where *kesi*, a similar technique, has a very long history. The designs on these tapestry-woven strips, however, reflect the Islamic love of geometric and stylized patterns rather than Chinese motifs.

Woman's tubular skirt (*malong landap*) of silk,
with silk tapestry-woven strips.
Philippines (Maranao people, Mindanao), 20th century
IS.40-1997

Contrasting Fabrics, Linings and Pockets

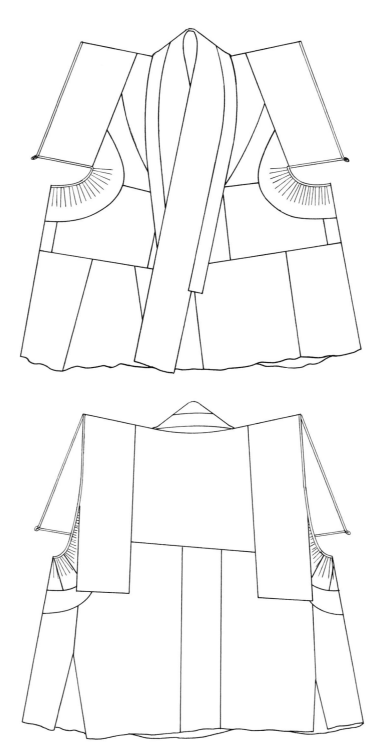

The elaborately pieced construction of this jacket recalls the patched robe (*kesa*) traditionally worn by Buddhist monks in many parts of Asia, although here the 'patches' are pieces of expensive Chinese and Russian silk and metal-thread brocades. This garment is part of a complete outfit that reputedly belonged to the last of the Yellow-Hat abbots of the Monastery at Tengyeling, Lhasa. He had been implicated in a plot to assassinate the thirteenth Dalai Lama and the monastery was closed down. The abbot's costume also includes a long wrapped skirt, a scarf, a sleeved inner jacket of buttercup-yellow corduroy, a wallet and flask, a pair of high felt boots and one of the distinctive tall yellow woollen head-dresses that gave the sect its name. The flamboyant projecting shoulder of this jacket is typical of Tibetan monks' outer garments and is outlined with elegant blue silk piping.

Tibetan abbot's outer jacket of wool,
with silk and metal-thread woven panels.
Tibet (Lhasa), late 19th or early 20th century
IM.92c-1930

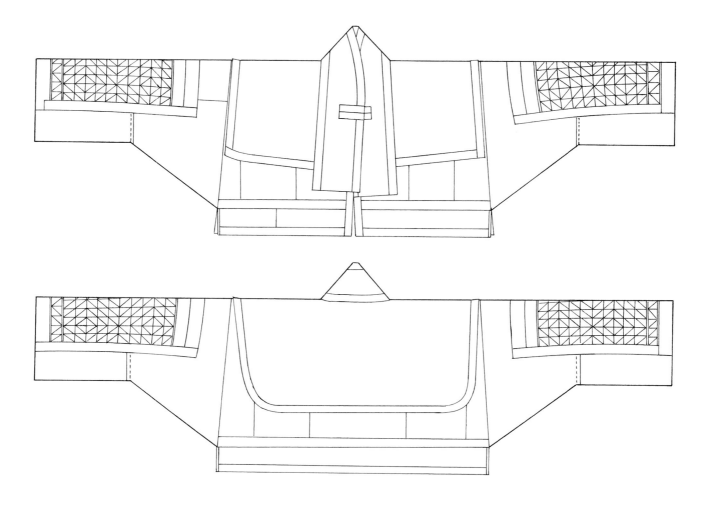

The detail here shows a pieced section of a jacket that was made and worn in the south-west of China by the Miao people. It is the back part of the sleeve. The entire jacket is fashioned from pieces of silk, cotton and wool, some of which are densely embroidered. Separate pieces of material, later made up into jackets, were easier for women to pick up and work on as they moved about their homes doing domestic chores. The part pictured is, in effect, a patchwork within a patchwork. The detail shows triangles of different coloured plain and yellow-spotted resist-dyed cotton as well as red striped wool. Arranged in a pattern of concentric diamonds, the patchwork is outlined with a broad band of red wool to which a zigzag stitching line in blue has been added. Folded appliqué strips, in bands of white, red and blue, mark the edge of the triangular patchwork section towards the shoulder. The many different techniques employed on this jacket attest to the versatility of its maker; all Miao clothes are showcases for several technical skills. The donor of this jacket was Britain's consul general for this area of China at the beginning of the twentieth century and he acquired the jacket himself from a woman who had reportedly taken two years to make it.

Woman's festival jacket in cotton, silk and wool.
China (Miao people), early 20th century
Given by Mr B.G. Tours
T.78-1922

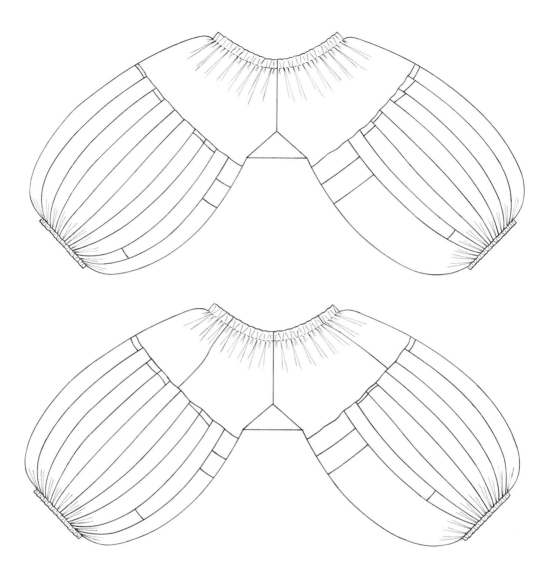

Fine blue cotton, which can be tightly gathered, has been used to form the upper part of these trousers. It re-appears at the bottom where it is gathered into cuffs at the ankles. In between a coarser, stronger blue cotton has been used – less suitable for gathering but undoubtedly harder wearing.

Coloured strips of fine cotton embroidered with a lace-like pattern in red and white and in red and black have been sewn together and then attached to the coarse cotton legs. The seams between the strips have been disguised by laying red or black silk threads along them and stitching them in place with white silk through both thicknesses of fabric. The small rosettes within the lace pattern were also embroidered through both thicknesses.

Pieced strips of block-printed cotton have been used on the inside of each leg, partly because they would not show and printed fabric was cheaper than embroidered but also because the inner leg is subjected to much wear and tear. If you look at the black strip to the right of the printed ones, you will see that a patch of plain black cotton has been sewn on top of the lower part. This is because the lower half of the embroidery has worn thin and torn in places. Printed strips along the inner leg would have been cheaper to replace than embroidered ones.

Women's trousers of cotton, embroidered
with silk and block-printed cotton.
Iran (Zoroastrian community), 19th century
IS.9A-1954

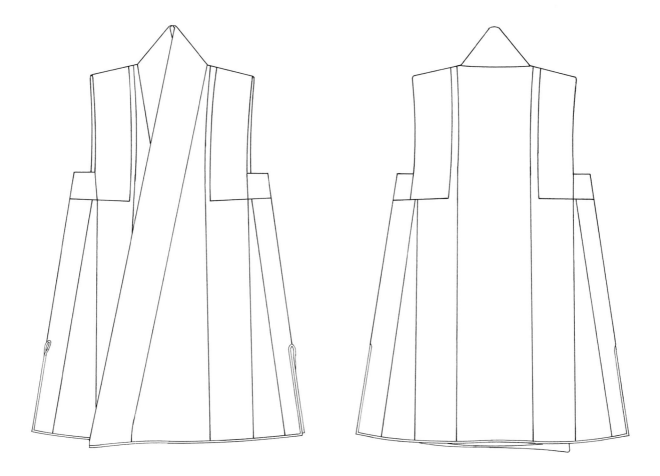

This coat is made of local felted woollen cloth, with panels of Chinese silk damask around the armholes. The deep red fabric is typical of garments made for Tibetan monks, but the cut of the garment does not conform to the usual monk's wardrobe, in which coats and jackets often have exaggerated shoulders (see p.117 for example). The use of striped cloth with painted crosses may also suggest that this is more likely to be a woman's outer garment.

Striped woollen cloth is traditionally associated with women's aprons, and the additional crosses have probably evolved from a type of woollen cloth that is patterned with irregular tie-dyed circles with cross-like motifs in them. The coat was acquired in Sikkim by the celebrated plant-hunter and botanist Joseph Hooker, who travelled in the Himalayan region between 1847 and 1851.

Woman's coat, wool with silk panels
Tibet or Sikkim, *c.*1850
Given by Dr (later Sir) Joseph Hooker
240-1869

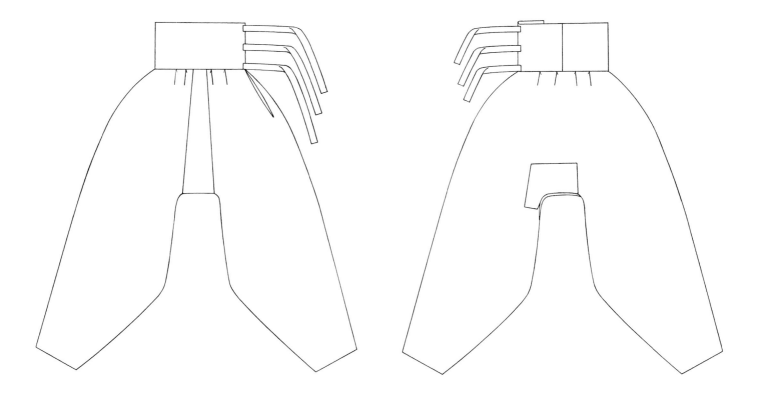

The artist Chunghie Lee (b.1945) makes great use of Korean patchwork techniques in her work. Stitched together with differently sized pieces of silk gauze, these multicoloured trousers were made to be worn with the dark turquoise jacket depicted on p.44. In Korea, patchwork was already being made during the Chosŏn period (AD 1392–1910), when it is especially seen on wrapping cloths (*pojagi*). Typical of Korean patchwork is the use of geometric shapes, worked together in intricate asymmetric patterns of contrasting colours. The women who traditionally made wrapping cloths and other items using patchwork techniques had no formal training, but instinctively created beautiful fabrics using old scraps of cloth. Customarily a Korean woman's dress consists of a short jacket with a long, full skirt fastened just below the breast. The shape of these trousers, however, imitates the pantaloons that women began wearing under their skirts during the Chosŏn period. With their wide waistband, side fastening and voluminous shape, the trousers closely resemble their earlier counterparts, yet the patchwork design, with its effect of contrasting colours and textures, creates a very modern feel to the garment. Pictured here is a detail from the lower right leg.

Woman's trousers of silk gauze.
Korea, 1995
By Chunghie Lee (b.1945)
FE.281:2-1995

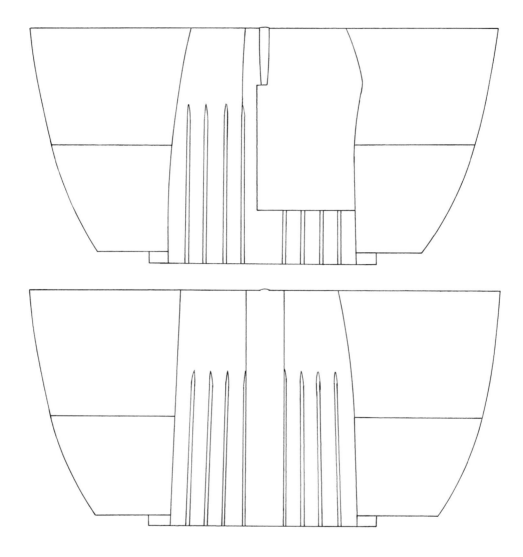

The large pieces of commercially produced cloth, probably imported, which have been used to make this robe are in sharp contrast to the narrow hand-woven strips which can be seen on pp.146 and 148. The time required to construct this garment would have been reduced because of the greater width of the fabric but any saving made here might have been offset by the cost of using imported goods. Fewer seams do not necessarily mean less cost.

The vertical inserts from the hem hardly alter the shape of the robe, adding only a very slight curve, but the tailor turned them into a decorative feature by introducing different fabrics. The main fabric of the robe is a white cotton woven with a pattern of small dart-like triangles. The inserts have been cut from white cotton of similar weight, woven with different patterns. From the left, the first insert has a large zigzag pattern; the next has a smaller-scale zigzag, which is followed by an insert with a pattern of leaves and the right-hand insert has been cut from the same fabric as the robe. This insert has been turned so that the design lies in a different direction.

The woollen threads used for the embroidery were only loosely twisted and have relaxed giving a matted effect rather like felt.

Man's robe of cotton embroidered with wool.
Northern Nigeria (Hausa), early 20th century
Circ.125-1966

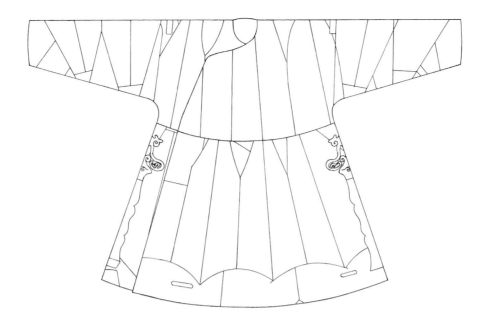

Sixty Pacific salmon, each weighing between 6.8–9kg (15–20 pounds), were used to make this coat. Their skins have been sewn together with sinew, using the natural shape of the salmon to create a subtle decorative pattern of seams. The front of the coat is plain but the upper back is covered with a patchwork of overlapping, scale-like panels each decorated with applied skin. The smooth inner side of the salmon skin has been used for the appliqué and has been painted red, black or blue and been stitched in place using coloured silk.

This coat is unlined and there are no fastenings at the front, suggesting that it was unused when acquired by the Museum. Similar garments in other collections often have three metal buttons which fasten into leather loops and sometimes they are lined with cotton. The skins of animals, in this case fish, make effective wind- and rain-proof garments which can be vital to human beings who live in dangerously cold environments. They are also an effective and inventive use of natural resources.

Woman's marriage coat of salmon skin.
Russia (the Amur Basin, eastern Siberia), c.1900
626-1905

This skirt belonged to a woman of the Banjara community. The Banjara (also sometimes called Lambadis or Lambanis, among many other local names) are an itinerant group who were formerly bullock-transport carriers to the Mughal army and, later, the British. Now that improved road and rail transport have made them redundant in that sphere, they are often employed in road and building work, with the women dressed in distinctive, brightly coloured clothes like this skirt (and the matching blouse shown on p.206). The use of appliqué and mirror embroidery are typical of the Banjara women's dress: this one uses mirrorwork at the waistband as well as a variety of applied fabrics to decorate the hem. These include factory-made striped shirt material and a simple printed cotton fabric to line the inside of the hem.

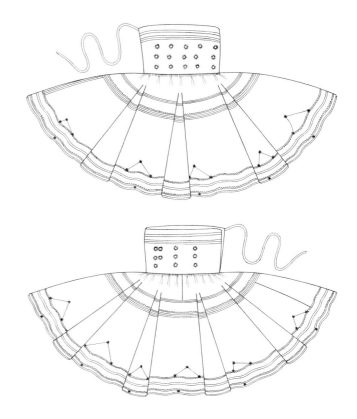

Woman's skirt of cotton, embroidered, printed and appliquéd.
India (Karnataka)
Acquired in Bidar, Karnataka in 1932
Given by K. de B. Codrington
IM. 47-1933

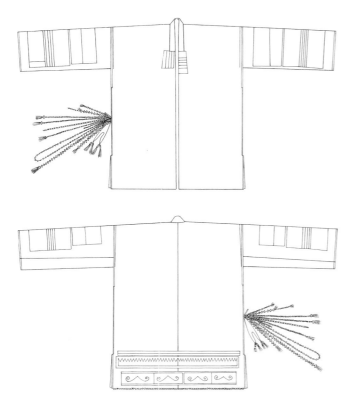

This subtly decorated jacket is part of an ensemble that includes a gathered skirt, separate leggings and a tall hat decorated with beads. It was made by a woman of the Akha tribe. The Akha originally came to Burma from Yunnan in south-west China, and a Chinese influence is evident in the scrolling appliqué work in these panels at the bottom of the back of the jacket. Much of the decoration of the jackets of these hill tribes is on the reverse of the garment (see also p.108) while the front is left relatively unadorned. This one is also decorated with two long, swinging ropes of beads and seeds which hang at each side.

Woman's jacket of cotton with appliqué and beaded tassels.
Myanmar (Burma), (Akha tribe, Southern Shan State),
early 20th century
Given by Mr R. Grant Brown
IM.77-1922

This panel of fabric is applied to the back of a man's jacket from eastern Burma. The woven silk is Chinese and the printed floral material is European, probably English. These two imported fabrics, sparingly used as decoration on this rather plain jacket, make a striking contrast to the traditionally Burmese cut of the garment. The panel cuts across its two contrasting halves, the upper one of plain dark blue cotton and the lower one patterned with a dense, red woollen woven design. Cowrie shells are used to highlight the decorative panels. These are a common auspicious decoration on garments in many parts of Asia. A corresponding panel on the front of the jacket is placed in two halves on either side of the unadorned front opening.

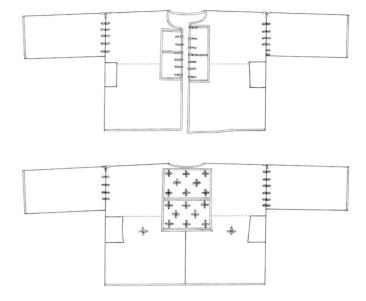

Man's jacket of cotton, with silk and cotton panels, applied
cowrie shells and wool.
Myanmar (Burma), (Akha tribe, Kengtung, Shan State),
late 19th century
IM.147-1929

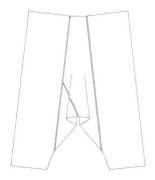 

Trousers began to be widely adopted in South-East Asia with the spread of Islamic culture across the region, often replacing local wrapped waist-cloths like the sarong. These short, loose trousers show the influence of the Persian and Turkish *shalwar*, although the bold striped silk fabric is more typically Malay. The waistband, which has two neatly bound slits through which a tie would be threaded, is lined with a European printed cotton fabric, which makes a striking contrast to the striped silk. European, especially English, printed cottons were favourite fabrics for linings and decorative trimmings throughout India and South-East Asia during the nineteenth century, often in combinations that seem incongruous to us today (see also the jacket above).

Man's trousers of silk with cotton lining.
Malay Peninsula, mid 19th century
05647 (IS)

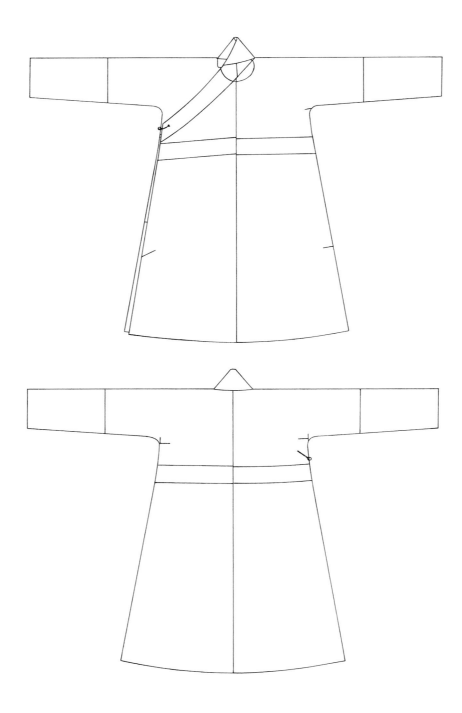

The striking lining of this Tibetan robe is made from two different silks. A deep blue silk with a design of Buddhist motifs is edged with red silk bearing cloud bands and dragon roundels. These rich red facings seem to have been especially favoured in Tibet. The scale of the designs on these lining silks is small and contrasts with the large-scale dragon motif curling up the front and back of the outside of the garment. This yellow dragon silk as well as the blue and red lining materials were all woven in China, a regular source of fine textiles, not only for Tibet, but also for other Himalayan Buddhist states. This Tibetan robe echoes the design on dragon robes worn in China by male officials of the imperial bureaucracy and it would have played a similar role in Tibet. The wearer is likely to have come from one of Tibet's noble families who were obliged to reside in the capital, Lhasa, to carry out government duties. This detail shows the inside of the front overlap section that fastens across the chest.

Man's robe of dragon-patterned silk.
Tibet, 19th century
T.96-1966

Japanese *kimono* often have striking linings which are tantalizingly glimpsed at the hem as the wearer walks along. Some linings are not designed to be seen at all, but to wrap the wearer in secret luxury, auspicious motifs or in designs that reflect her or his personal taste. In this *kimono* the delicate design of plum blossoms on the outside contrasts with the bold combination of lime green and bright red on the inside. The green silk has been woven with a pattern that represents rippling water, the curving shapes echoed in the outline of this fabric on the red crepe which is embroidered in gold

with scattered flowers. *Kimono* are more correctly known as *kōsode*, which means 'small sleeve', a reference to the opening at the wrist. The sleeves on this example are very long, indicating that it would have been worn by a young, unmarried woman. It has a large padded hem and was designed as an outer *kimono* for winter wear. The plum motif is a popular design for such *kimono* as this tree is the first to bloom in the new year. The theme on the lining, of blossoms falling by a riverside, is also suggestive of the coming pleasures of springtime.

Woman's *kimono* of woven silk, lining of woven silk
and embroidered silk crepe.
Japan, second half of the 19th century
Given by T.B. Clark-Thornhill
T.78-1927

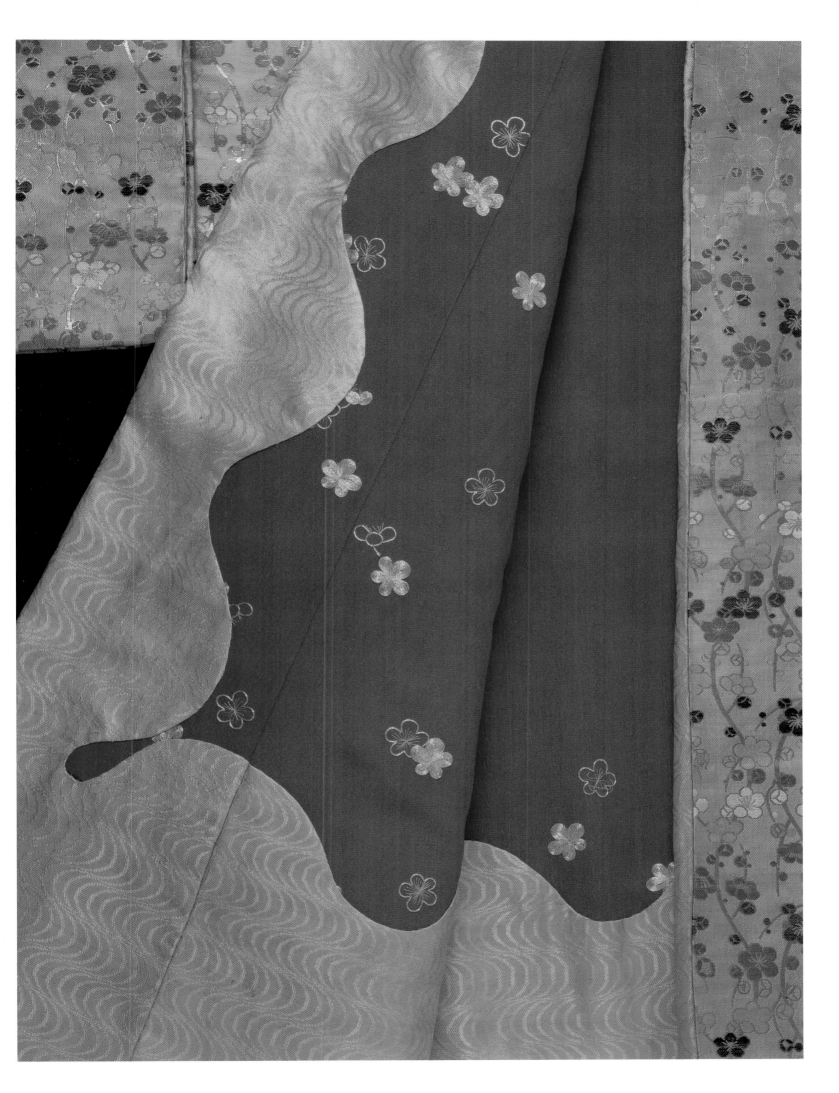

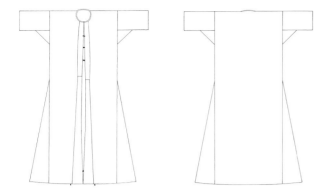

This is a lining which does little to support the shape of the garment or to make the wearer more comfortable but it does create a quite unexpected effect on the right side of the coat.

On the inside edge, there is a facing made from diagonal blocks of silk and then there are dozens of silk squares, some slashed along their sides and some with holes roughly chopped in them. Each square has been turned to form a diamond, lined up on the diagonal and oversewn with red silk. The stitches holding them in place have been taken through to the right side of the coat where they form a strong and irregular pattern of adjoining diamonds.

There are no fastenings and so the front panels would have opened as the wearer moved, revealing some, but by no means all, of the silk patches.

Woman's coat of cotton embroidered with silk.
Galilee, late 19th or early 20th century
T.242-1966

The prevalence of bright silk linings on garments of this type suggests that the buttercup-yellow damask on this one was meant to be glimpsed when the coat was worn. The coat itself is side-closing. The fastenings only reach to the waist, leaving the lower section open at skirt level. The lining might well have been exposed here and at the armholes, which are particularly capacious to accommodate the robe worn underneath. These sleeveless outer coats were a feature of Manchu women's dress (see p.79). Many of them are dark blue or black on the outside and have applied decoration also in blue. The colour may have been a conscious fashion choice to distinguish it from the long-sleeved robe beneath. The lining, taken right up to the very edge of the inside, provides a third colour contrast.

Woman's sleeveless coat of embroidered silk.
China (Manchu), 19th century
T.127-1966

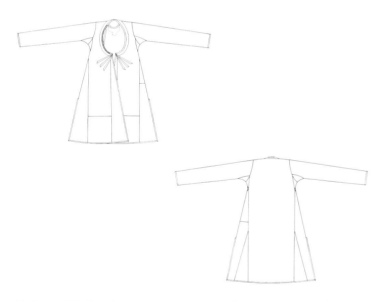

Linings of Indian luxury garments are often given as much attention as the surface fabric. They may be in a striking contrasting colour or, as here, in a patterned fabric that complements the outer design. In this case, the repeat floral pattern is in gold on the outer fabric, while that of the lining is in a softer, yellow floss silk. The use of a broad border in a third fabric (here, plain red) is also typical of northern Indian courtly wear. This may be a Central Asian tradition, as it is used to great effect on the ikat robes from that area. The front of this garment is illustrated on p.13.

Man's robe (*angarkha*) of silk with gold-wrapped thread.
Pakistan (Sindh), mid 19th century
05648 (IS)

Time was of little consequence in the making of this coat. It is a large garment with strangely cut sleeves. The only way they make sense is if the coat is worn draped over the shoulders or over the top of the head and the sleeves hang down the wearer's back.

Every inch of the coat has been covered with floral stripes embroidered in cross stitch. A tablet-woven band has been sewn on as an edging and the large red silk stitches holding it in place can be seen around the edge of the silk lining. Not only was the vast expanse of embroidery time-consuming to produce but the four-coloured resist-dyed (ikat) lining required three separate dyeing processes after which some of the panels were glazed to make them darker and more reflective.

Coat of cotton embroidered with silk and lined with silk ikat.
Uzbekistan, second half of the 19th century
T.61-1925

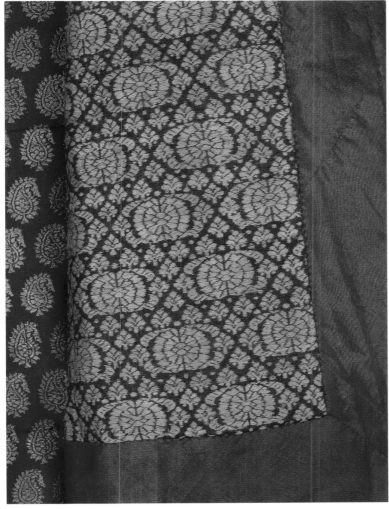

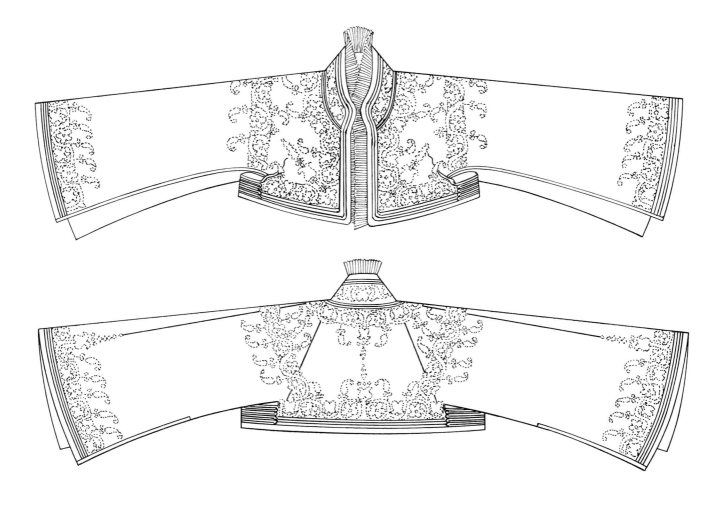

Imagine the softest, silkiest velvet one side and the coolest, smoothest satin on the other. The combination is slightly squashy as if it were padded and your instinct is to brush first one side and then the other against your cheek to experience contrasting textures so close together. This is a sensual marriage of fabrics and ought to be worn next to the skin. However, it has been constructed into a jacket, to be worn over at least one layer of other clothing. Although its self-indulgent qualities are lost on the wearer, it enchants the eye and the imagination of the observer.

The cream silk lining is a high-quality dress fabric woven with a delicate pattern of leaves and flowering stems. There is no added colour, just a combination of weave structures which reflect the light in different ways. In contrast, light sinks into the purple velvet and is absorbed by it. Couched metal thread can be glimpsed in the lower right-hand corner (see also p.18) and while it has reflective qualities, its hardness is rather unsympathethic.

It is possible that the lining is not original and was added after the jacket had been brought to England.

Woman's jacket of silk velvet embroidered with metal thread.
Bosnia and Herzegovina, *c*.1880
Given by George Hubbard and purchased by him in 1884.
T.178A-1928

Stamping patterns onto cloth was a traditional decorative technique in northern India and Iran. It was done with heated metal clamps, and was often applied to cotton or silk garments to give a lattice pattern to the material. This would be re-done after washing. The same technique was applied to fabrics woven with metal threads, and the resulting patterned fabric of silver or gold was used in several types of northern Indian garment, usually used in linings or edgings, as here. This elaborate pattern of flowers within a diamond shape is derived from a seventeenth-century Mughal design, which would have been used as decoration on architecture and metalwork as well as textiles. The front of the same piece is shown on p.183.

Lining of a head-covering (*odhni*) of cotton and silver filament.
India (Delhi), *c*.1869
803-1869

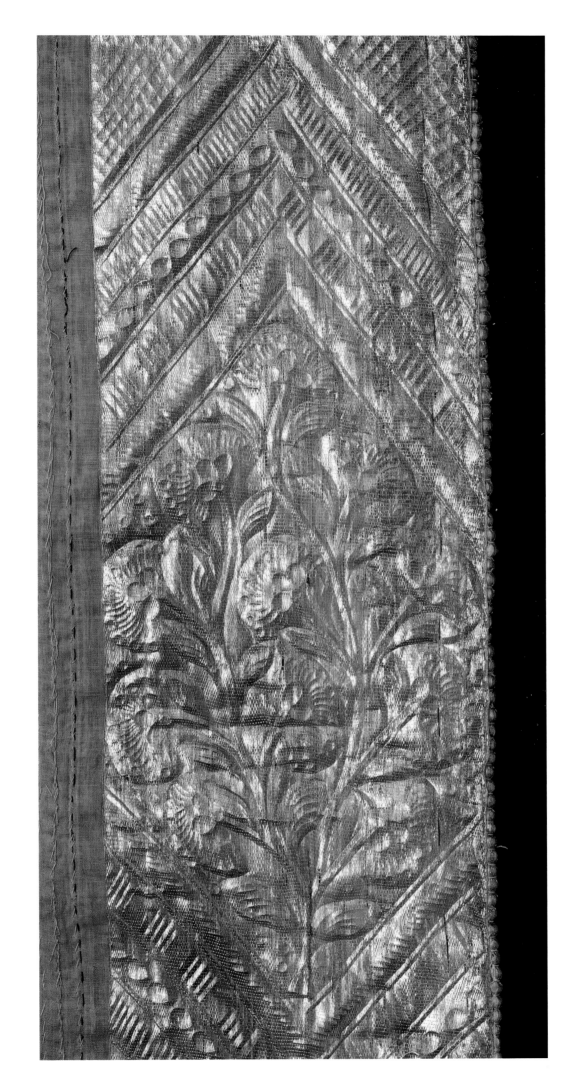

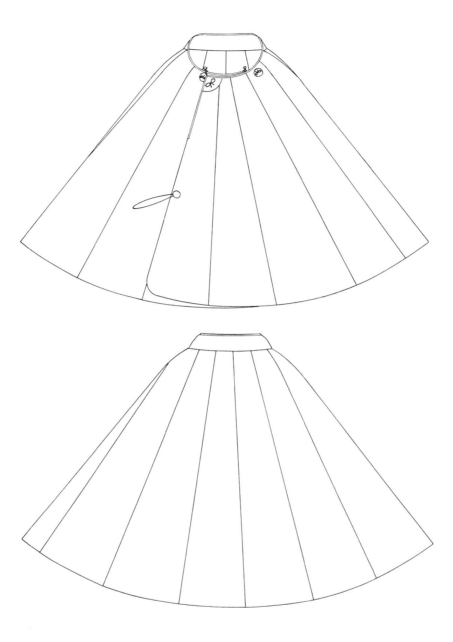

Indigo-dyed cotton fabrics are synonymous with everyday life in nineteenth-century Japan. On this cape the popular blue dye has been used on both the outer and inner fabrics. One side has been patterned with the *kasuri* technique, in which the yarns are selectively dyed prior to weaving. The other side is elegantly striped in blues, black and orange. The garment is known in Japan as a *bōzukappa* and is constructed from sixteen triangular sections of cotton with a short upright collar fitted at the neck. The style was adapted from capes worn by Portuguese missionaries in Japan in the sixteenth century, the name deriving from *bōzu*, the Japanese for 'priest', and *kappa*, the Japanese transliteration of the Portuguese for 'cape'. The wearing of such capes was originally restricted to members of the military *samurai* class, but by the eighteenth century other sections of society had adopted it as a travel garment. The cape is reversible and it was apparently common to wear the striped fabric on the outside. The inner fabric would be revealed when the cape was worn with the sides folded back. The garment could also be worn overlapped at the front, protecting the traveller when it was cold and windy.

Man's travel cape (*bōzukappa*) of woven cotton.
Japan, second half of the 19th century
FE.1-1988

Two thicknesses of blue and white cotton have been used to form the body of this robe while the sleeves, which need to be easily folded back and draped, are made from one thickness.

The embroidered decoration on such large robes is traditionally concentrated on the large pocket that covers the left breast. In this example the design was drawn in brown ink and then embroidered with green silk. The most easily discernible motifs are those decorated with massed eyelets, each small hole oversewn with silk to prevent fraying and producing a flat, pock-marked surface. The horizontal band across the top of the pocket and the five daggers hanging from it are worked in pattern darning with the silk thread forming a flat pattern of small diamonds. This design is not immediately obvious but shows more clearly with the interplay of light in movement.

At the corner of the pocket is a curved insertion which secures and reinforces the part most vulnerable to wear and tear.

Man's robe of cotton embroidered with silk.
Northern Nigeria (probably Hausa), late 19th century
Anonymous Gift
T.699-1994

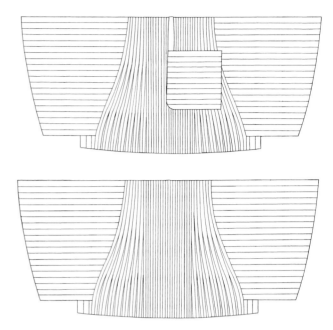

Pockets imitating the circular openings of European watch-pockets enjoyed a fashion in northern India during the second half of the nineteenth century, and are seen in all sorts of male coats and jackets. It has even been suggested that the shape has some religious significance, the crescent moon being a symbol of Islam. However, it is much more likely that this attractive detail owes its popularity in India to the strong influence of European styles on formal male dress. The rest of the coat is in the style of a northern Indian closely fitted coat such as the *achkan* or its close relative the *chapkan*, both of which button down the front.

Young man's coat of white cotton with applied silk braid decoration and printed cotton facings.
Northern India, mid 19th century
8261 (IS)

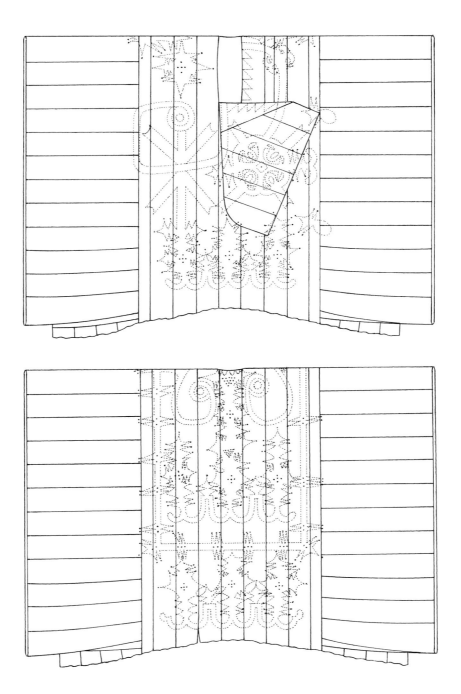

It is difficult to comprehend the scale of this garment: the strips of indigo-dyed cotton from which it is made are only 11cm (4 inches) wide, yet the width across the shoulders is 185cm (73 inches). The width of the sleeve openings is 135cm (53 inches) – designed to allow cooling breezes to reduce the discomfort of a hot climate.

The pocket illustrated here is very large and is placed over the left breast. It is the main focus for concentrated embroidered decoration. Its upper corner has been turned back and secured with embroidered zigzags to form the lower edge of a rectangular neck opening, the double thickness providing some strength to the part which will receive greatest wear. The embroidery is worked in minute running stitches with details in chain stitch and small eyelets. Although it is centred on the pocket, it spills over onto the rest of the robe, linking with other embroidered elements.

The size of the pocket and the fact that the embroidery extends beyond it makes it less obvious as a functional pocket, but when worn the front layer of fabric would have sagged a little, making its presence more obvious.

Man's robe of cotton embroidered with silk.
Mali (Mandingo), 1880s
Said to have belonged to a chief named Bashir-el-Beiruc who
lived in the desert between Cape Juby and Sageit-el-Hamara.
Given by Najib Kisbany
1110-1898

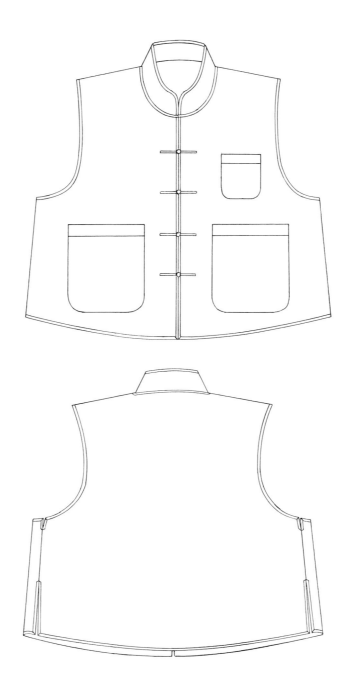

Chinese garments did not originally have pockets like these but, by the beginning of the twentieth century, they were being added to traditional styles. This was a time when Chinese men started wearing western three-piece suits or a mix of Chinese and western modes. This waistcoat is made from closely woven black ribbed silk and it has a subdued pattern of lattice roundels woven into it. The pockets have been tailored to ensure there is no break in this design. The match across the sewing lines is meticulous as is that across the fold-line at the top of the pocket. This waistcoat has shoulder seams and the back is cut from one piece of cloth, which, like the pockets, are a sign of twentieth-century tailoring. Sleeveless jackets like this were usually worn over long robes and the slits at the sides allowed for expansion. The garment is versatile enough to be worn with western clothes and this may well have been how it was used. It was part of the bequest left to the V&A by Sir John Addis and, as a diplomat in China, he seems to have had several Chinese-style garments made especially for him.

Man's waistcoat of black patterned silk.
China, mid 20th century
Bequeathed by Sir John Addis
FE.129-1983

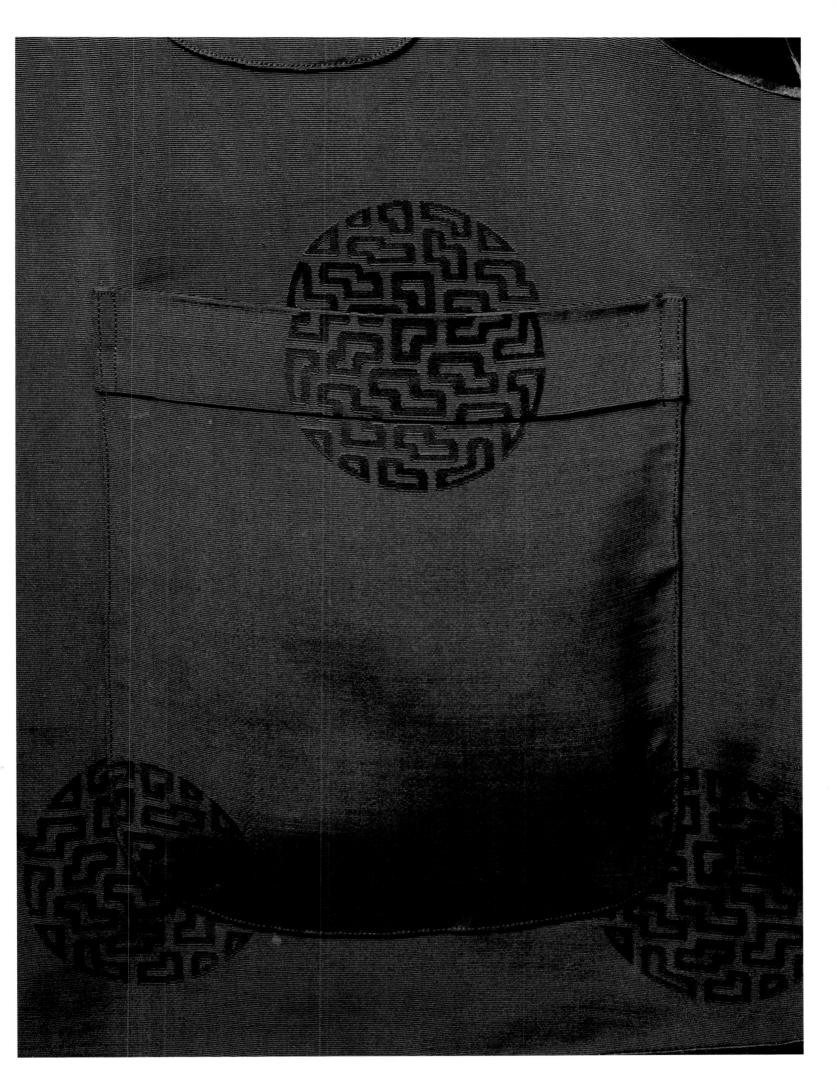

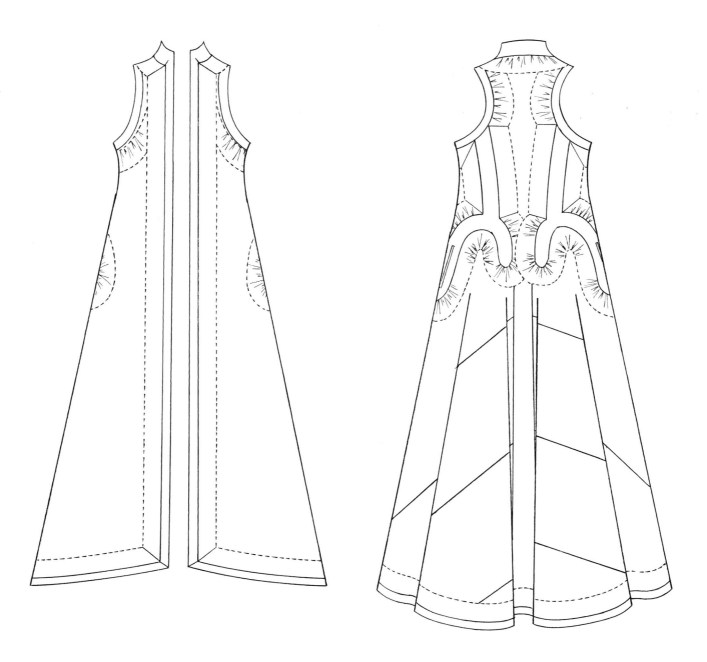

At first glance the way this coat is decorated seems so uncompli-cated and so simple in comparison with the more intricately pat-terned garments in this book that one might think the maker had cheated. Woven braid runs around the edges and covers most of the upper back as it sweeps down and around the hips, encircling the slit which allows access to a pocket in the underlying garment. Apart from several rows of silver cord which follow the same con-tours and are sandwiched between the braid, there was no further attempt at adornment.

But look again at the 'simple' attachment of woven braid. It has

a weft in which a flat silver strip has been closely wound around a yellow silk core. While this creates the pattern and the glitter, it also makes the braid stiff and relatively inflexible. It is easy to stitch this along the straight edges of the coat but here the maker applied it around the neck and armholes and, more dramatically, allowed it to follow the natural curves of the pelvic girdle. This required mitre-joints at the corners and tight, secure gathering along the inner curves. Neither is as simple as it might seem and both have been achieved with great skill.

Woman's sleeveless coat of woven silk with brocaded details,
trimmed with applied metal braid and cord.
Bosnia and Herzegovina, second half of the 19th century
Given by H.C. Game
T.142-1928

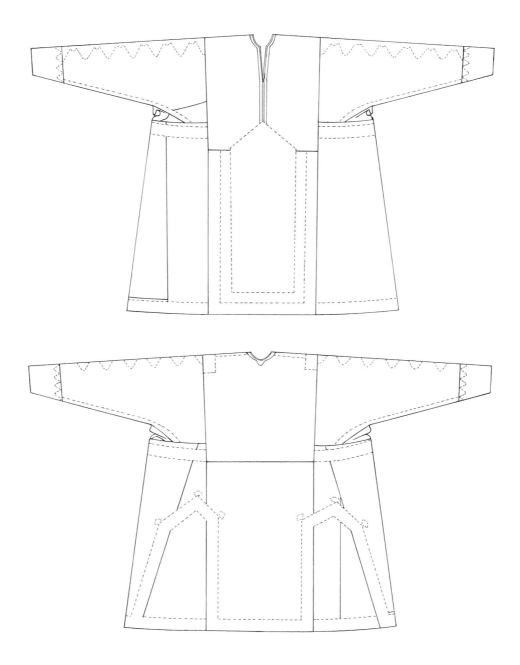

Baluchi women's dresses (see also pp.68, 112) are characterized by the extraordinarily long front pocket that runs from waist level almost to the hem. The pocket is embroidered in the same designs as the two front panels of the *pashk,* while the rest of the dress has very little ornamentation. The back of the dress is made of a coarser, more durable fabric than the fine silk or cotton used for the main part of the garment. It may seem very impractical to have a single huge pocket in which one's possessions are indiscriminately jumbled together, and this does lead to considerable rummaging on the part of the wearer. Money and small items such as keys are usually carried in a more accessible manner, tied up separately in a small bundle at the waist or knotted into a corner of the wearer's head-covering.

Woman's dress (*pashk)* of cotton embroidered with red silk thread.
Pakistan (Baluchistan), early 20th century
T.42-1912

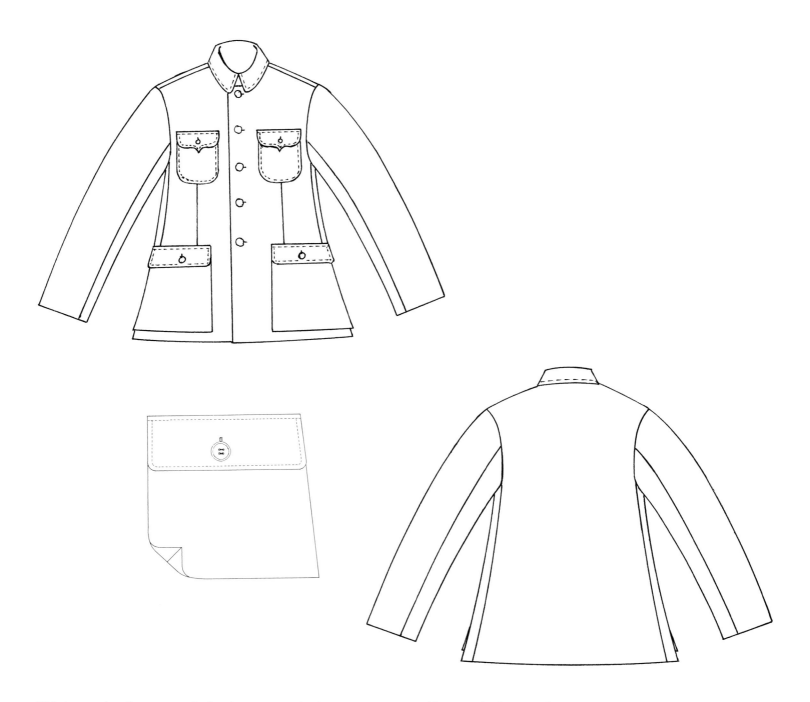

This is a pocket from an outfit that has come to be known in the west as a Mao suit. The style is associated with the iconic figure of Mao Zedong (1893–1976) who favoured it partly because of its capacious pockets. Two small breast pockets, each with a curved, buttoned flap, and two larger pockets at waist level are perhaps the features which best define this trouser suit. Furthermore, the lower pockets are distinctive in that they are expandable. The section of fabric forming the pocket is first folded under around the edges to a depth of 2cm (1½ inches). The pocket is not sewn to the garment along this fold-line but further inside, allowing for its expansion.

Not everybody wore the Mao suit during Chairman Mao's leadership (1949–76) and, among those who did, there were variations in fabric, fit and colour. It continued to be worn after his death, less so as the years went by. This suit, for a woman, was made at the Red Flag Factory in Shanghai. A European visitor purchased it off the peg at the Department Store in Beijing. She wore it during her stay there in the early 1980s to blend in with the general population at a time when an international style of dressing was only just becoming acceptable in Chinese cities.

Woman's Mao suit jacket of cotton and polyester mix.
China, 1980
Given by Carl and Rosemarie Samuelson
FE.1:1-1997

Pleats and Gathers

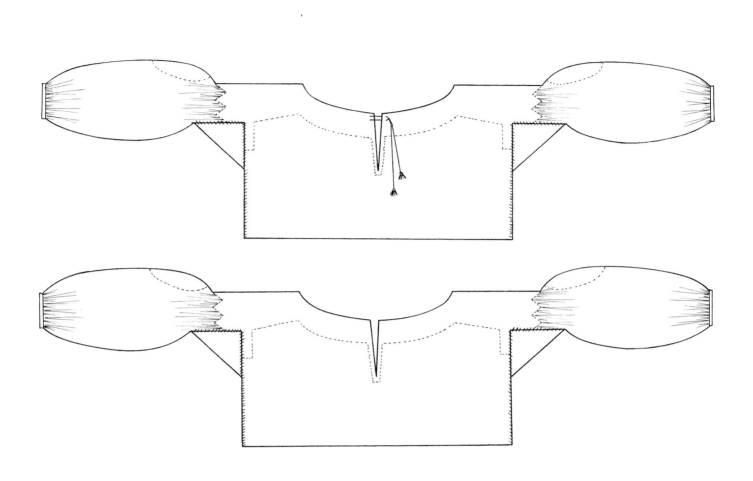

In the small area across the width of one shoulder, four very different embroidery techniques have been combined. Running along the ridge of the shoulder and then extending around it is a band of white linen zigzagged lines on a background of red silk. Running along either side of the shoulder ridge are panels in which only the background has been embroidered, leaving the pattern in reserve – the plain white linen cloth of the blouse forming small flowers (see p.164). Below these panels are isolated motifs embroidered with thick silk thread and around the top of the sleeve are tiny gathers, which are held in place by pink silk threads, visible only if the gathers are gently teased apart. Thick red silk has been used to embroider a pointed design directly on top of the gathers. This ensures that they stay in place but the upward-pointing gathers and the downward-pointing embroidery also form an interesting pattern.

Because the fullness of the sleeve begins well below the shoulder joint and because the shoulders themselves are embroidered with small flat stitches, the wide and rather shallow neckline seems to have been extended. As well as being pretty, this blouse would have had the added advantage of creating width in line with the wearer's breasts while making her neck appear long and slender.

Woman's blouse of linen embroidered with silk and linen.
Spain (Andalusia), 19th century
Given by Mrs Willoughby Hodgson
T.205-1916

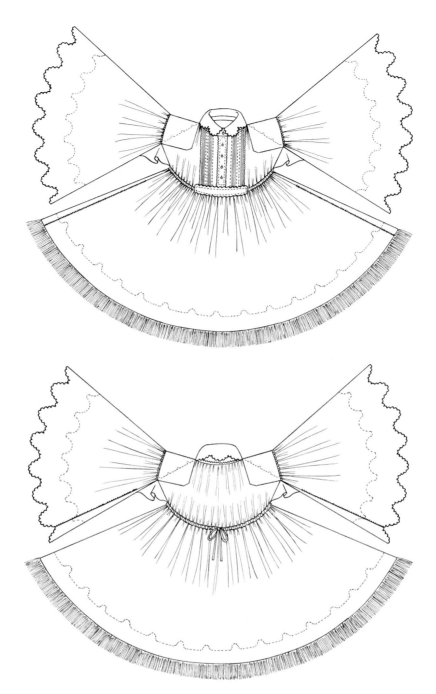

Without precise tailoring it is difficult to combine fullness and close-fit in one garment. The problem has been solved in this boy's shirt by using concertina-like pin-tucks to reduce the fullness across the chest, combined with loose gathers over the shoulders and a drawstring around the waist. The pin-tucks and the gathers change the character of the otherwise unremarkable cotton cloth by adding textures and shadows to disturb its smoothness.

To a certain extent this three-dimensional quality is then balanced by the addition of flat satin-stitch embroidery in red, orange and purple cotton. The narrow vertical rows nestle within the pin-tucks while the more prominent central row (with orange pearlized buttons) and the waistband are softened by a pointed edging of needle lace. The collar, which is slightly overshadowed by the exuberant decoration across the chest, introduces another textural element by using eyelet embroidery to change the very nature of the cloth.

This shirt, like one from Paraguay (see p.26), was worn over a pair of straight, undecorated cotton trousers. Trousers are subjected to constant movement and pressure and cotton ones in particular have a limited life span, so it makes sense to apply skill, care and creativity to shirts that are more visible and longer lasting.

Boy's shirt of cotton embroidered with cotton.
Hungary (Mezőkövesd), second half the 19th century
73-1903

The linen may be discoloured with age but the skill and attention to detail with which this small blouse was made is still evident and astonishing. Comfort and freedom of movement were assured by using ample amounts of linen for the body and sleeves but controlling it at the neck and wrists by gathering it tightly and securing it with lines of decorative stitching with black silk. The addition of a gusset under the arm would allow the child greater movement.

Instead of using simple seams, the sleeves and gussets have been attached with embroidered insertions. Worked with linen thread between the pieces to be joined and imitating lace, these insertions create a light and delicate balance to the volume of fabric falling from the neck. A similar effect has been achieved along the top of the shoulder by pulling together threads from the linen ground and securing them with white and light brown silk.

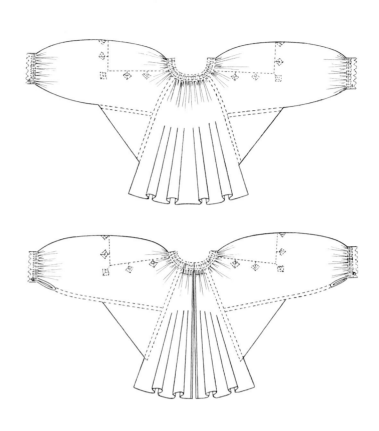

Child's blouse of linen embroidered with silk
with linen insertions.
Spain (probably Murcia), 18th century
Anonymous Gift
T.144-1924

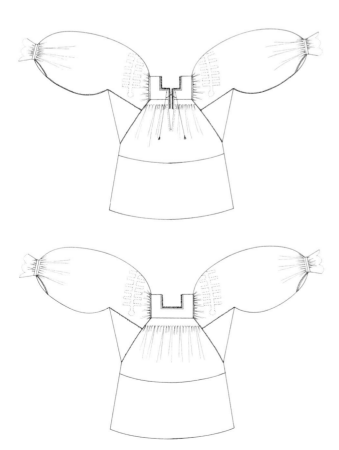

Given the popular association of Spain with bull-fighting, it is fitting that bulls, albeit large-eyed spotted ones, should be embroidered around the square neck of this blouse, which has been completed with a woven upholstery braid. Two holes have been punched along either side of the neck opening and a plaited cord has been threaded through and is used to fasten the front opening.

The linen sleeve and the linen which forms the main part of the blouse have been gathered and decorated with embroidered bands and then attached to the edges of the embroidered neck panel. The gathers on the sleeve are not at the top of the arm but run across the shoulder at the point where the collar-bone joins the shoulder blade. This, together with the many gathers running above the breasts would have created a rounded, inflated appearance, made more obvious by the contrast of the neat, flat embroidered band around the neck.

Woman's blouse of linen embroidered with silk.
Spain (Andalusia), 19th century
Given by Miss D.M.E. Car
T.41-1973

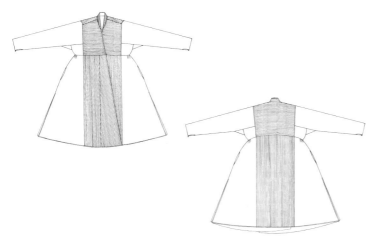

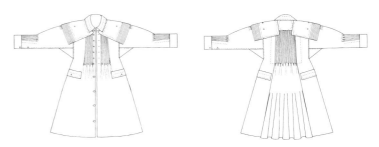

The work of the Indian designer Asha Sarabhai and her studio, Raag, focuses on simplicity of design, materials and decoration, with texture often playing a dominant role in the treatment of the fabrics. This woman's coat has front and back panels stitched into minute pin-tucks, which give a very subtle texture, rather like the gills of a mushroom. This is the only decoration on this beautifully understated garment, which is an adaptation of the shape of a loose robe (*choga*) of Central Asian origin, traditionally worn mainly by men in northern India.

Woman's coat in a mixture of silk and wool.
India (Ahmedabad, Gujarat), *c*.1995
Designed by Asha Sarabhai for Raag
IS.18-1995

Were it not heavily embroidered this would be a working garment for an agricultural labourer. The extent and elaboration of the decoration suggest it was not for everyday wear, but was probably reserved for special occasions. It is made from cotton twill – a strong, durable fabric; the same weave is used to make denim jeans.

The most distinctive features of the smock are the two large panels of double thickness which extend over the shoulders and the upper arms to provide a little extra warmth and protection and to encourage rain to run off rather than soak through to the body. The outer edge of each panel was divided into bands and every alternate one was embroidered with a zigzagging line. The fabric was then folded and stitched so that the embroidered bands overlapped the plain ones, forming a heavy and attractive layered border. Three pearl buttons attach the panel to the shoulder of the smock.

Man's smock of cotton twill embroidered with cotton.
Southern England, late 19th century
Bequeathed by Emma Ehrman
T.109-1998

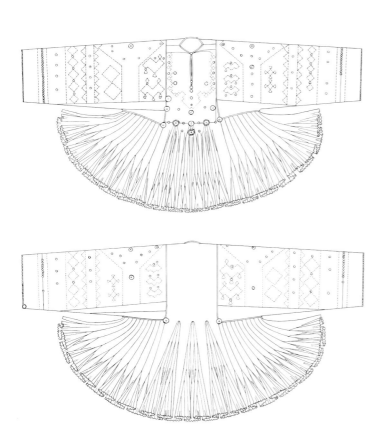

This woman's dress from Northern Pakistan has an astonishing 524 triangular and rectangular panels inserted into the skirt to provide a swirling mass of fabric around the knee-length hemline. The use of prodigious amounts of cloth is also a feature of other types of dress from this region, for example the immensely wide-waisted trousers formerly worn by both men and women. It is not clear whether this taste for extra cloth is a response to the harsh climate in this remote mountainous region or a form of modesty that hides the outlines of the legs. Another detail of this dress is shown on p.209.

Woman's dress (*jumlo*) of twill-woven cotton embroidered with silk thread and with applied buttons and other decoration.
Pakistan (Indus Kohistan, North-West Frontier Province), mid 20th century.
IS.33-1996

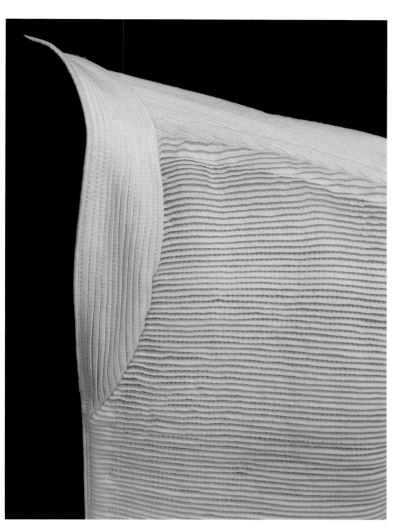

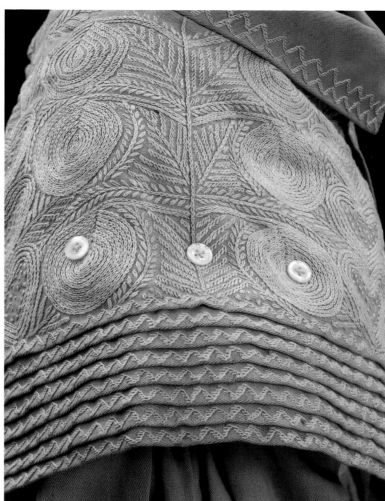

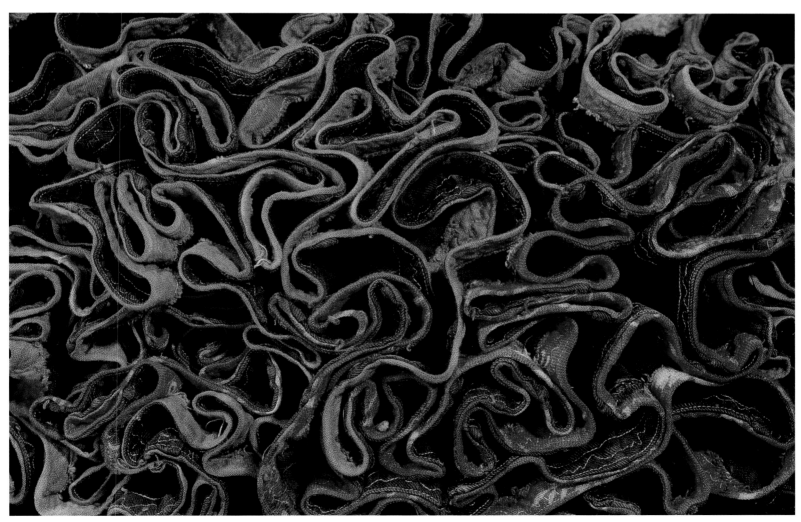

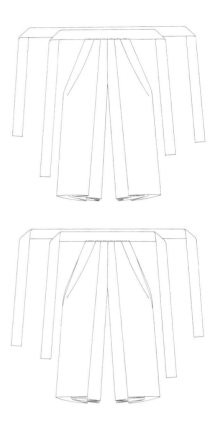

Pleated *hakama*, variously described as full-cut trousers or a divided skirt, are an important item of dress for both men and women of the Japanese imperial court and for men of the *samurai* (military) class. There are various types of *hakama*, but they all share a similar basic shape (see pp.196 and 212). Like most items of court dress *hakama* are loose and voluminous, serving to enhance the presence of the wearer by expanding the area they occupy. They are wide with broad pleats and taper towards the top, being secured with bands that wrap and tie around the waist. The sides are open half-way down, revealing the robes worn underneath. This is an example of *nagabakama*, or 'long *hakama*'. When worn the hems would have trailed under the foot and out behind giving the impression that the wearer was constantly kneeling. They would have been worn by court nobles or high-ranking *samurai* on very formal occasions.

Man's court trousers (*nagabakama*) of woven silk.
Japan, 19th century
Given by T.B. Clark-Thornhill
T.68-1915

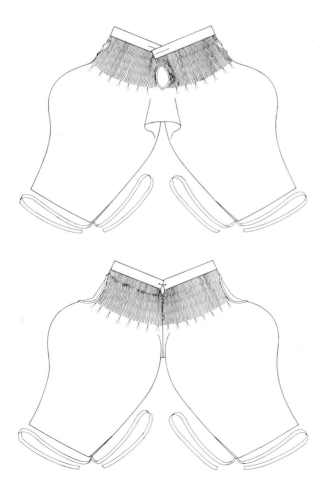

Looking like ripples on a sandy beach after the tide has retreated, these tight gathers are incredibly beautiful – as you stare at them they seem to shift in and out of focus, the faint horizontal steps become more prominent and the whole image seems to shimmer like a heat haze. They are simple gathers but the effect of so many, so close together, in strong, thick linen is fascinating.

On the inside it is possible to see eight lines of linen stitches which hold the gathers together and create the slight stepped effect. The stitches at the top, nearest to the waistband, are tight and close together. Those towards the bottom are very slightly looser, allowing a little movement and presumably letting the breeches fit more comfortably around the hips.

Man's breeches (*bragon bras*) of linen.
France (Department of Finistère), *c.*1820
16B-1902

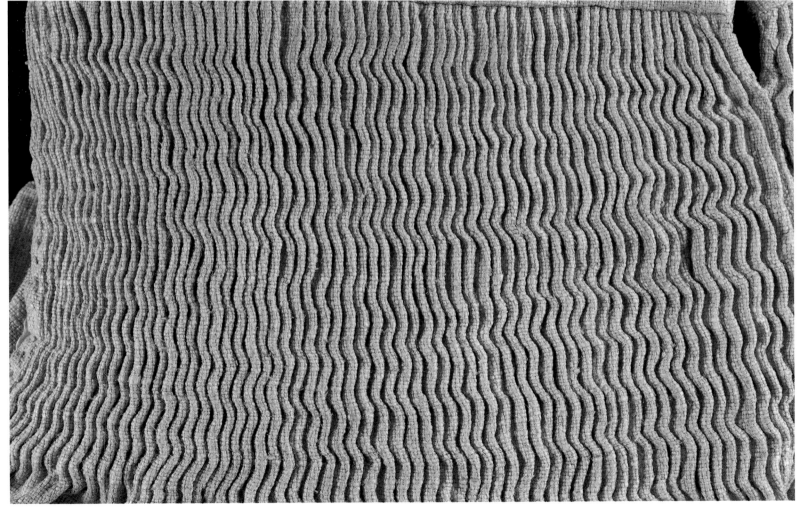

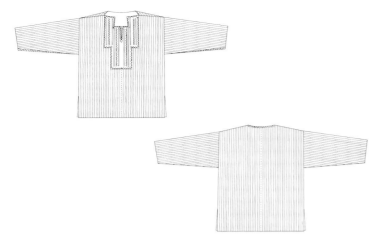

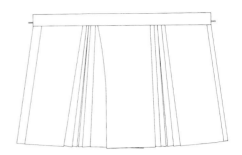

The naturally golden sheen of Indian *tasar* silk is used to dramatic effect in this woman's shirt from Asha Sarabhai's studio. Although the boxy shape of the shirt and the permanently sewn flat pleats may not be traditional features of Indian dress, the use of appliqué strips of triangular decorative edging is often seen in regional dress and textiles in Gujarat, where this piece was made. This edging would traditionally have been in cotton fabric of a contrasting colour (usually red), and its much more subtle use here is typical of the more subdued aesthetic of this contemporary workshop.

Woman's shirt of *tasar* silk.
India (Ahmedabad, Gujarat), *c.*1995
Designed by Asha Sarabhai for Raag
IS.21-1995

Hemp is not the weight of material that necessarily lends itself to fashioning pleats. This type of wraparound skirt is more usually made from silk, which does pleat well, so it seems the traditional style held sway whatever the fabric. The detail shows one set of six pleats, arranged in two groups facing the centre of the panel. Each pleat is stitched vertically along its folded edge in the manner of a French seam. All of them are held in place with a horizontal line of long, light blue stitches indicating that the skirt has never been worn. There is no decoration here and the garment derives its beauty from the handle of the fabric and its rich indigo-blue colouring. Historically, hemp was a major textile fibre cultivated and processed in China. It was ousted by cotton as the main material for everyday wear but is occasionally used today.

Woman's skirt of hemp.
China, 20th century
Valery M. Garrett Collection purchased with funds from the
Friends of the V&A
FE.213-1995

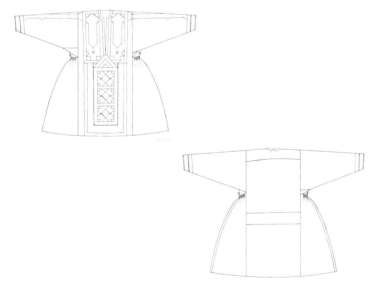

Although the traditional Baluchi woman's dress is extremely voluminous, it is invariably made with ample pleats and gussets under the arms to ensure ease of movement and to minimize strain on the sleeve seams. This vibrantly coloured shot-silk dress has beautifully stitched pleats under the arm feeding into the gathered material of the skirt. It is common for underarm gussets in India and Central Asia to be accentuated by being made of a different, often brilliantly coloured, contrasting material – a feature that is also found in linings and the inner facings of hems.

Woman's dress (*pashk*) of silk with silk embroidery.
Pakistan (Baluchistan), mid 19th century
6060 (IS)

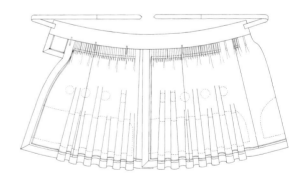

The pleats on this court skirt are evenly arranged along the entire length of the waistband. In Chinese, this style of box pleat is called *bi ji* which translates as 'piled-up pleats'. A double row of running stitches secures down the pleats to a depth of 6cm (2½ inches) from the top. Above these stitching lines the pleats lay flat while, below the lines, they flare out, adding bulk to the wearer. Like the skirts for Chinese women, this one wraps around the body and has embroidered decoration on the lower section towards the hem. The waistband, while it is unlikely to have been seen, is, nevertheless, woven with a dragon roundel design. It is made from an extremely stiff silk and the ties at each end are of the same material.

Man's court skirt of embroidered silk.
China, 18th century
T.251-1966

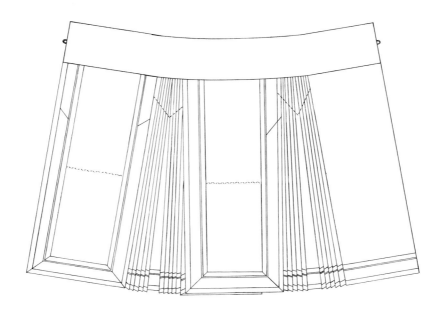

This detail shows one pleated section of a panelled skirt. When worn, it is wrapped around the body in much the same way as a kilt. The pleats swing out to either side as the wearer moves. The Chinese woman who wore this skirt probably had bound feet and would have swayed from side to side accentuating the swing. It is likely that Chinese women wore these skirts around their hips rather than right on the waist; the pleats fall more gracefully if the skirt is not pulled in at waist level. The pleats are held down at the top in a V-shape with simple running stitches. This gives some elas-ticity to the pleats and ensures that they swing well. There are twelve pleats in each pleated section. Six are folded over one way and six the other so that each group faces into the centre. Every individual pleat is defined with narrow bias-cut black satin which is left plain near the top part of the garment, and is covered with embroidery, in shades of blue, on the lower third. A tiny, flat gold-woven edge further enhances each pleat. It is only the lower part that will show beneath the three-quarter-length gown that was tra-ditionally teamed with this style of skirt.

Woman's skirt of embroidered silk.
China, second half of the 19th century
Given by Miss Baxter in memory of Miss Kate Baxter
Circ.771-1912

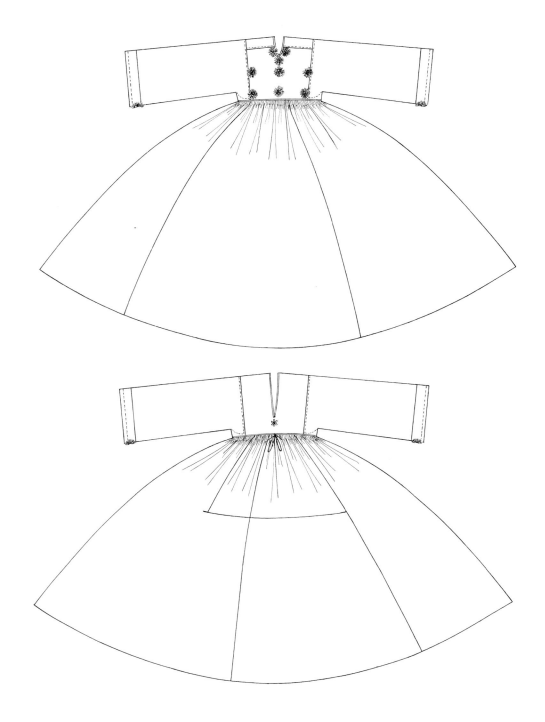

This brilliantly striped gathered fabric is from the back of a woman's dress from the Afghan-Pakistan border. The main part of the dress is made of plain black cotton, with a panel of colourful embroidery on the chest. It is usual for embroidered dresses to have a patch of thicker, durable material on the back, and whereas these are usually of a plain and often drab material, here a vibrantly striped material has been used. The usually unadorned back has also been further decorated with a simple embroidered star of metal-thread ribbon (*gota*).

Woman's dress of cotton, embroidered with silk thread.
Afghanistan/Pakistan borders, mid 20th century
IS.140-1965

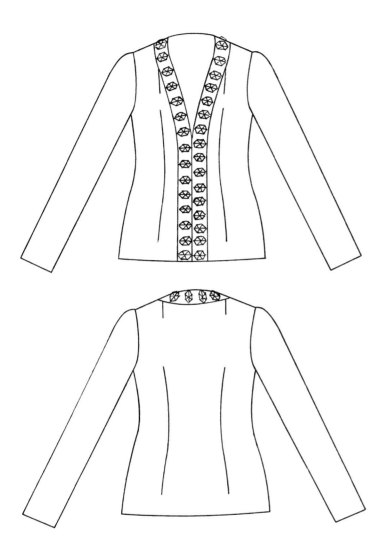

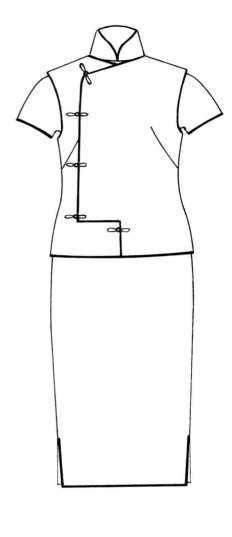

This ruching goes along each side of the jacket front opening and around the neck. It is made from one long strip of silk, cut on the cross, and first fashioned into evenly spaced inverted pleats. The two open ends of each pleat are then teased towards the middle and fixed together with a small stitch. Each of the resulting twenty-five ruches looks like a small, attached bow. The edge to edge jacket can be fastened in place with hooks and eyes, which are discretely sewn just inside the garment. This brings the two sides evenly together and shows off the tucked edging to good advantage.

Alternatively, the jacket can be left open to reveal a matching waistcoat with decorative frogging in dark red. The third part of the ensemble is the dress itself, made from the same patterned slub silk and tailored in the *cheongsam* style (see p.25). The jacket band, manipulated into crenellations, adds depth to the outfit. It accentuates the layered effect, produced by wearing three garments, one on top of the other. This ensemble is an example of how the *cheongsam* form can be adapted and re-worked to suit a particular customer or occasion.

Woman's jacket of printed silk, part of a three-piece ensemble.
China (Hong Kong), 1950–60
Given by Richard A. and Janey M.Y. Cheu
in memory of Dr Henry D. Cheu
FE.55-1997

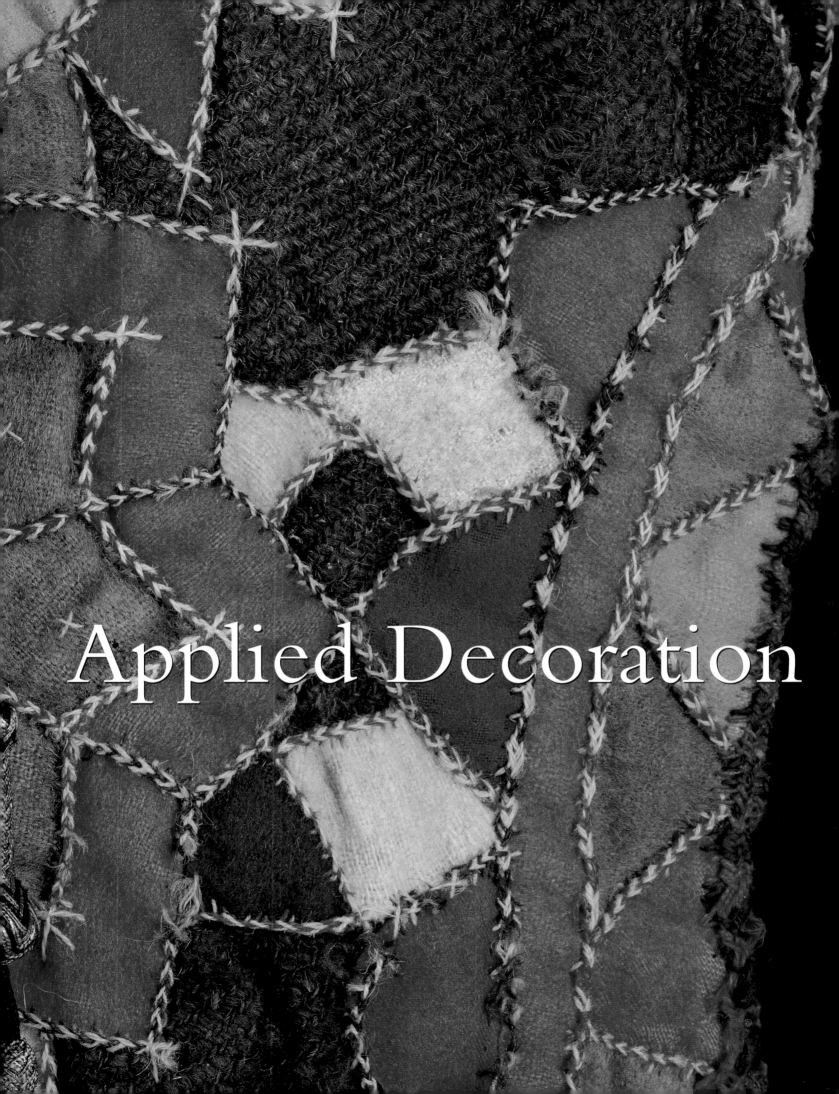

Applied Decoration

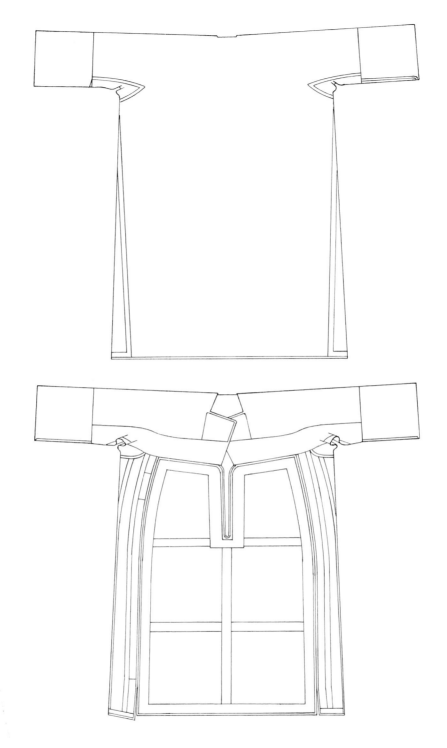

This woman's tunic was made by a woman of the Lohana farming community in the arid plains of Sindh, in southern Pakistan. These densely embroidered garments are made for weddings, but are also subsequently worn as part of everyday wear to indicate the wearer's married status. The stiff, embossed style of embroidery is particularly associated with the village of Thano Bula Khan, and this distinctive work is used on smaller items such as caps and bags as well as on these elaborately decorated shirts. The rigid effect of the embroidery is also increased by the addition of pieces of mirror-glass into the embroidered surface. The back of the garment is divided into six panels, each less solidly embroidered than the front, and is therefore more flexible.

Woman's shirt (*chola*) of silk embroidered with silk and cotton
thread, gold-wrapped thread and mirrors.
Pakistan (Thano Bula Khan, Sindh), mid 20th century
IS. 16-1974

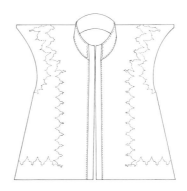

A great deal of dress in India is based on a simple rectangular shape draped around the body (whether head, torso or waist) rather than being cut and sewn into body-shaped garments. This woman's head-covering is simply a long piece of cotton decorated with applied metal ribbon (*gota*) formed into leaf shapes and sewn on to the cotton ground. It would have been worn draped over the head and cover most of the upper body, together with a matching outfit of a full skirt and bodice. The lining fabric is shown on p.143.

Woman's head-cover (*odhni*) of yellow cotton, with applied decoration in coloured cotton fabric and pleated gold ribbon (*gota*), lined with stamped metal-thread fabric
India (Delhi), *c.*1869
803-1869

The couched silver-wrapped thread decorating this boy's jacket suggests Chinese influence, although the black woollen ground fabric has overtones of European military costume, which is echoed in the decoration of the front of the garment. The island of Nias, off the west coast of Sumatra, assimilated some of the finery of the courts of coastal Sumatra, but also had its own unique and elaborate range of ceremonial garments and ornaments. The extended shoulder-line of this jacket is typical of male dress in south Nias, and it would have been worn either on its own or over a long-sleeved jacket, with a loincloth or, more recently, western-style trousers. The jacket is lined with European printed cotton.

Boy's jacket (*baru*) of black wool flannel, decorated with couched metal-wrapped thread.
Indonesia (Nias), late 19th or early 20th century.
IS. 44-1997

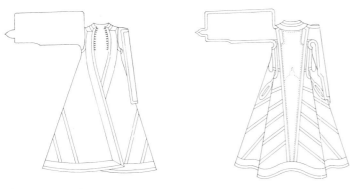

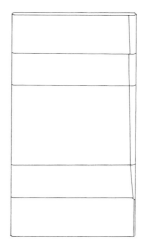

The ground of this red velvet coat has been divided into sections by rows of silver cord which alternate with thinner gold ones. These encircle the opening which gives access to a generous pocket – one on either side of the coat. It is almost impossible to see the red velvet ground beneath the convoluted lines of metal thread which ooze into every corner, rather like the creeping tendrils of a weed, feeling its way through gaps and filling the available space.

Two colours of metal thread have been used: small amounts of a reddish or coppery gold outline the silver cords while the rest of the embroidery is worked with glittery yellow gold. Both types of threads have been produced by winding flat metal strips around a yellow silk core.

Woman's coat with hanging sleeves, silk velvet embroidered with metal thread and trimmed with metal braid and cord.
Albania, second half of the 19th century
Given by Lieutenant Colonel C. de S. Luxmoore
T.46-1934

This type of simple tubular skirt is worn on ceremonial occasions by women of the Paminggir people of southern Sumatra, and is elaborately decorated with silk embroidery and tiny pieces of reflective brass. The figurative designs of the panels of fine floss-silk embroidery recall the woven ship-cloths from the same area, although this type of skirt more often has panels showing squid-like creatures rather than ships and humans. The use of bands with simple embroidery and small pieces of brass or mirror-glass has here replaced the more usual weft-ikat panels.

Woman's ceremonial skirt (*tapis*) of cotton with silk embroidery and applied brass sequins.
Indonesia (Paminggir people, Lampung, south Sumatra),
mid 19th century
9057 (IS)

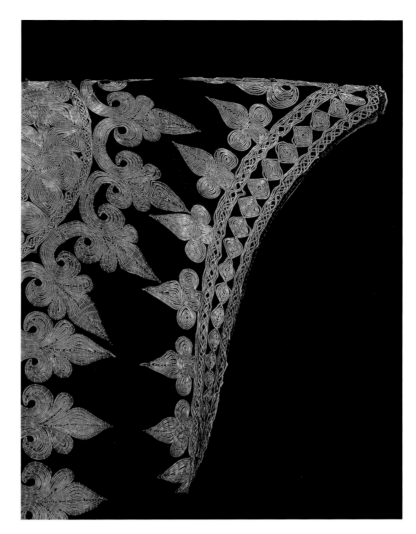

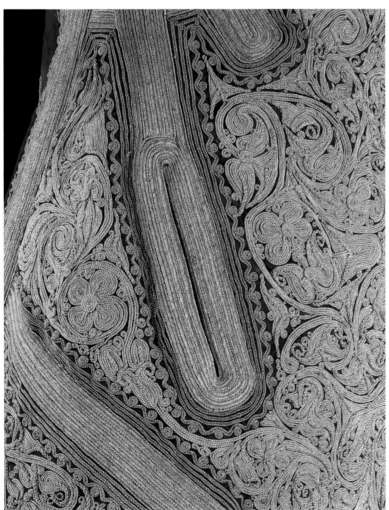

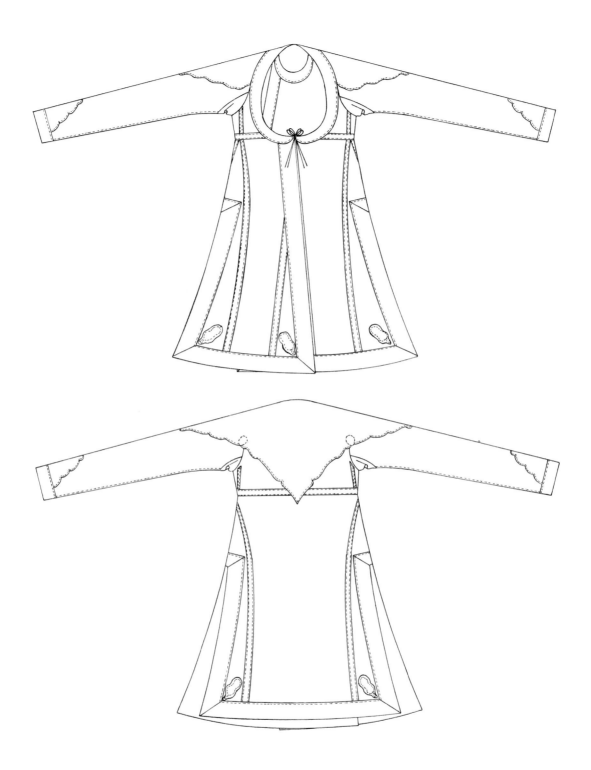

The circular shape of the neck opening, over a flat panel underneath, identifies this young man's robe as an *angarkha*, one of the most popular forms of traditional courtly or formal wear in northern India. This particular garment is unusual in that the elaborate gold-thread and silk embroidery has been done separately, and has been applied on to the ground fabric of the *angarkha*. The decoration around the back and shoulders is in the unusual form of a draped scarf, rather reminiscent of the 'cloud collar', a foliated decorative treatment of the neck and shoulders of some Central Asian garments.

Boy's robe (*angarkha*) of cotton, with applied panels of cotton
embroidered with gold-wrapped thread and silk thread.
Probably from Pakistan (Lahore), *c.*1855
5875 (IS)

This problematic but visually striking garment came into the Museum in 1948. It was acquired from a Swiss collector, Bernard Vuilleumier, and it was part of the biggest group of Chinese dress ever purchased by the Museum up to that time. The detail here is from the decorated yoke of the jacket. This goes around each shoulder, with white satin edgings outlining its foliated margins. Shaped black velvet and a band of orange velvet, painted with black stripes to resemble a tiger, add richness and lustre to the garment. The Museum records describe it as an imperial hunting tunic for a theatrical performance. Throughout most of the Qing dynasty (1644–1911), successive emperors made long excursions to their northern hunting parks to kill game, including tigers. During these hunts, foreign nobility, who did not live in Beijing, would renew their allegiance to the throne. Such presentation rituals might require clothes like the one here.

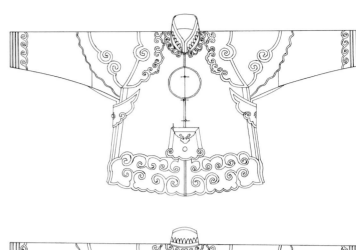

Man's jacket of embroidered and tapestry woven silk.
China, 18th or 19th century
Vuilleumier Collection purchased with assistance from the
National Art Collections Fund
T.186-1948

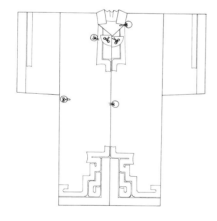

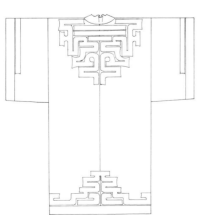

This robe was made by an Ainu woman in Hokkaidō, the northernmost island of Japan. The Ainu are an aboriginal people who live primarily by hunting and gathering. Their belief in the presence of spirits in every part of the natural world affects all aspects of their lives and is embodied in the textiles they make and use. Robes such as this are known as *attush*. They are made from fibres taken from the inner bark of the elm tree and worn by men performing the many religious ceremonies that take place in Ainu society. The robe has been decorated with pieces of indigo-dyed cotton cloth, which have been stitched down using an appliqué technique and then embroidered. The thorn-like motifs serve to protect its wearer from malevolent forces. This decoration is concentrated at the hem, shown in this detail, neck, cuffs and front openings to prevent evil spirits from entering at the most vulnerable points.

Man's robe (*attush*) of woven elm-bark fibre with appliqué (*kiri-fuse*) and embroidery (*oki-nuki*)
Japan, 19th century
Given by Bernard Leach
T.99-1963

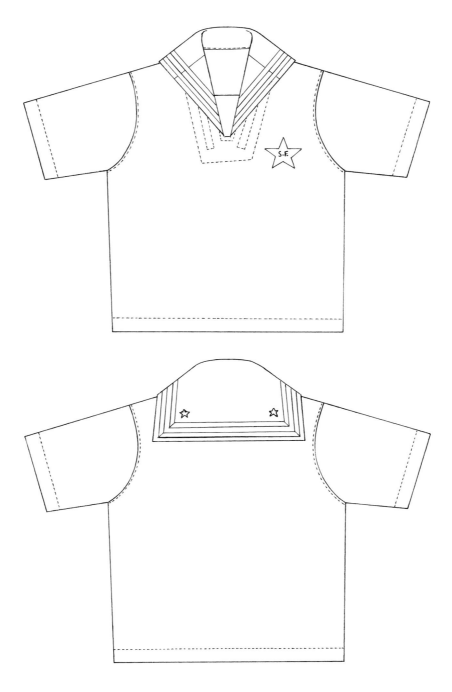

This is the logo for the Star Ferry of Hong Kong. It is emblazoned on the left breast of a seaman's top. The star is cut from strong, white cotton twill and machine-embroidered in blue with the initials 'S' and 'F'. This is then overstitched by machine onto the navy blue cotton twill top. On the reverse, the sailor collar has applied stars and bands, and the top is teamed with navy trousers, a navy knitted high-necked pullover and a white sailor hat with 'Star Ferry Co. Ltd.' written around the hatband in English and Chinese. This uniform is worn by seamen who operate the ferry service that crosses the water from the Central District of Hong Kong Island to Tsim Sha Tsui on the mainland; both areas are now part of the People's Republic of China. It takes ten minutes to cross over and the green and white boats of the Star Ferry Company ply the waters continually and relay thousands of passengers daily. The Star Ferry is very much enmeshed in local identity because it is seen as a distinctive Hong Kong phenomenon. This distinctiveness is partly generated by the tourist industry but it is a mode of transport genuinely used by local people in their day-to-day lives, one that they miss when they leave Hong Kong.

Man's top of cotton, part of a seaman's uniform.
China (Hong Kong), 1970s
Valery M. Garrett Collection purchased with funds from the
Friends of the V&A
FE.196:1-1995

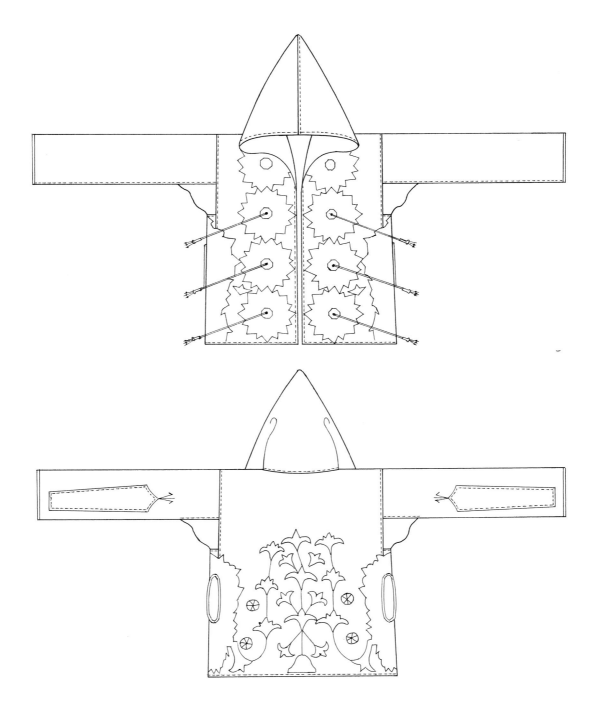

This functional but rough woollen garment, made from two layers of coarse wool, is one of several examples where bright, cheerful, often delicate patterns have been applied to what could be considered to be an unsympathetic fabric. In this case the back of the jacket is decorated with a surprisingly pretty floral arrangement of applied felted wool while the front is covered with applied eight-pointed stars, four on each front panel.

Each segment of the pattern has been outlined with red and yellow or blue and yellow stitching to conceal the joins. A star has also been applied to the upper inner side of each front panel so that when the hood is not worn and hangs down the back, the neck falls open to reveal more decoration. A pocket slit is visible along the right edge of the image and has been reinforced with blue and red stitching.

An elegant black silk and silver tassel hangs from the centre of each star and ends with a small coral bead, traditionally used as an amulet to ward off evil. These tassels form the only means of fastening the jacket.

A man's hooded jacket of wool decorated with applied felted wool.
Algeria, late 19th century
Given by Miss Gertrude Jekyll
T.117-1916

This silver flower decorates a dress worn by Alice Cheu (1914–79) in 1961. The dress, in the *cheongsam* style, was either tailored in Hong Kong or in San Francisco where Mrs Cheu settled. The garment is an example of a popular genre of *cheongsam* different from those with decorative fastenings and trims (see p.25). The only fastenings on this dress are unseen press-studs. The white satin is used as a surface for applied decoration rather than an expanse of silk to be framed with piping. A large spray of flowers, placed asymmetrically, curls down the front of the dress from the left shoulder across the skirt. The foliage was machine embroidered straight onto the satin. The flowerheads, the top one of which is pictured here, were made separately from satin offcuts and silver thread. The petals were stiffened with thin wire and only partially sewn to the dress. They were bent upwards to give a three-dimensional effect. This dress was worn at the wedding reception of Mrs Cheu's stepson in the United States; at her own marriage in Hong Kong she had also worn a white *cheongsam* but had pinned a corsage of real flowers, in the same diagonal shape as the silver ones here, to the shoulder of her wedding dress.

Woman's dress (*cheongsam* or *qipao*) in white satin.
China (Hong Kong) or USA (San Francisco), 1961
Given by Richard A. and Janey M.Y. Cheu
in memory of Dr Henry D. Cheu
FE.49-1997

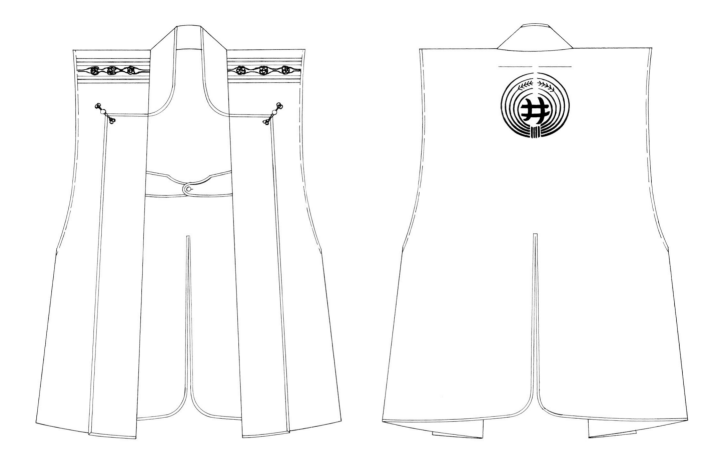

The art of silk braiding is known as *kumihimo* in Japan and has been used for many centuries to enhance the functional and decorative qualities of a variety of garments. Braiding has been used on this sleeveless jacket as both a form of decoration across the shoulders and to fasten the buttons holding the front lapels. The jacket is a *jimbaori* and was worn by a high-ranking *samurai* over his armour. *Jimbaori* developed in the sixteenth century but, by the time this example was made, Japan was at peace and such garments no longer needed to withstand the rigours of the battlefield. This *jimbaori* was worn purely for ceremony and was designed to reflect the status and power of the *samurai* class as well as the personal tastes of the warrior who wore it. It is made from imported wool cloth that has been treated and shrunk giving it a felt-like look and texture and lined with dark blue silk woven in gold with a dragon design. On the back in black wool appliqué is the *samurai's* family crest. The extravagant epaulettes, one of which is shown in this detail, are constructed of layers of stiff paper covered with stencilled deerskin, gold wrapped cord, black and purple wool and the blue braid.

Man's jacket (*jimbaori*) of wool with lining of
woven silk and applied silk braid and stencilled deerskin.
Japan, first half of the 19th century
T.136-1964

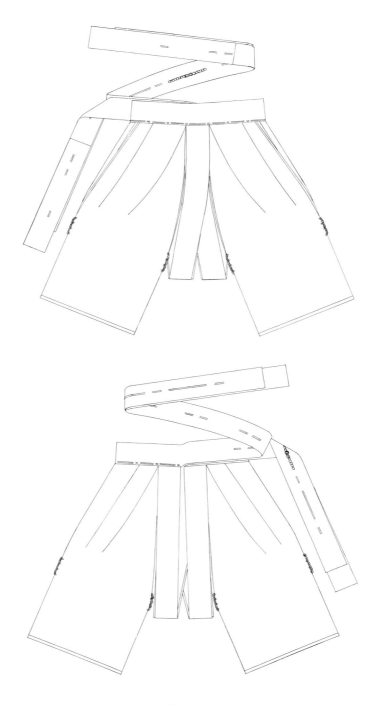

White cords of twisted silk have been used to enhance this pair of nineteenth-century Japanese hakama, a type of garment variously described as full-cut trousers or a divided skirt (see pp. 168 and 212). This pair are outer hakama and would have been worn as part of the most formal attire of the emperor, princes and senior nobility of the Japanese imperial court. This type of costume features two pairs of hakama, each pleated slightly at the top, open at the upper sides, and tied around the waist with broad bands. The outer pair is always of white silk woven with a pattern of floral roundels often,

as in this example, of wisteria. The lining is of red silk, which shows at the sides, hems, bands and on the two unusual broad loops that mask the opening at the crotch. The edges of this lining have been treated and feel like paper. This may have been done to reinforce vulnerable areas of the cloth. The laced double cords at the top of the side seams also serve this purpose. Pairs of cords, threaded through side by side and tied in places in elaborate knots, have been used to decorate the long waist bands.

Man's court outer trousers (ue no hakama) of woven silk with
threaded silk cords.
Japan, 19th century
Given by T.B. Clarke-Thornhill
T.66-1915

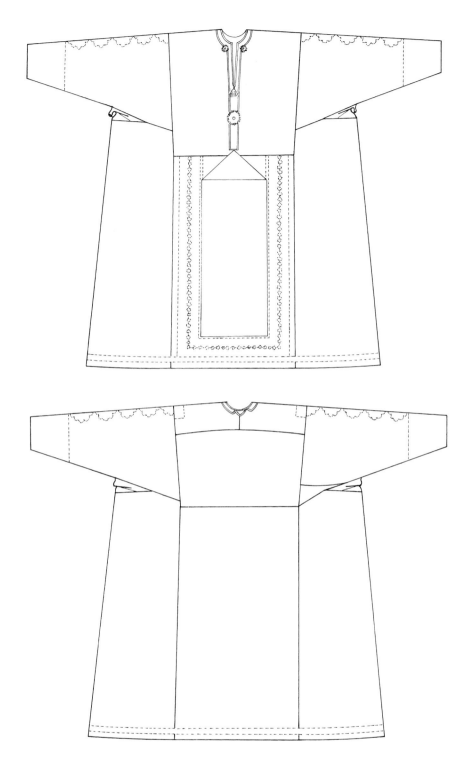

Women's dresses from Baluchistan in Pakistan are traditionally embroidered on the front with densely worked panels of embroidery. Unlike dresses from other parts of Pakistan, they rarely incorporate any extra applied decoration, but occasionally, as here, they are embellished with decorative tassels or tufted silk pompoms around the neck-opening. The embroidery on Baluch dresses varies according to region, and this extremely fine, monochrome silk embroidery is influenced by the similar work of Kandahar, just across the border in Afghanistan.

Woman's dress (*pashk*) of cotton embroidered with silk thread.
Pakistan (Baluchistan), early 20th century
Given by Mrs Anna Whitehead
IS.32-1969

The side of the hip is not the most obvious place for this three-dimensional decoration but its purpose may have been to draw attention to a wide pelvis, eminently suitable for child-bearing.

The coat is made from prickly wool, which had been woven and then dyed blue. The white specks which can be seen clearly are where small clumps of dirt or dust attached themselves to the fabric and did not absorb the dye. Red felted wool has been used to trim the edges of the coat and to form a broad band running from the back of the shoulder down to the hip and from there in narrow stripes to the hem. The large rosette placed on top of the hip bone is made from a disk of felted wool to which red, green and yellow tabs have been stitched. The red stripes have been edged with silk embroidery and white silk cords have been coiled and stitched into place. More coils run along the back edge of the decoration with a green rosette running diagonally into the small of the back – emphasizing again the roundness and power of the pelvis.

Woman's sleeveless coat of wool embroidered with silk and
trimmed with applied strips of woollen cloth and metal sequins.
Montenegro, c.1850
This once belonged to the orientalist painter Carl Haag
(1820–1915).
T.321-1921

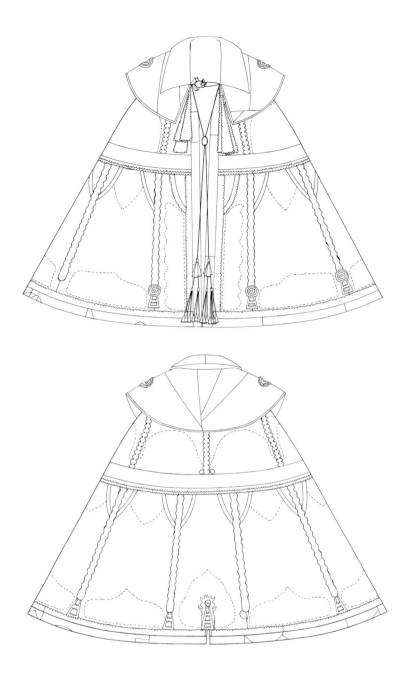

In the nineteenth century Hungary was justifiably proud of its furriers' art and this floor-length sheepskin cloak decorated with patchwork, appliqué, embroidery, tabs and tassels illustrates how skillfully tough leather can be worked. It requires great strength and was always an occupation for men.

Three techniques are illustrated in this image: patchwork, embroidery and appliqué. A strip of blue leather, embroidered with a meandering stem of leaves and flowerheads, has been inserted into the natural brown leather which forms the cloak. Sprays of stylized flowers and leaves have been embroidered onto the brown leather

using satin stitch, with the silk thread being taken all the way through the leather and back again. The scalloped band of leather running across the lower end of the picture has been applied on top of the brown leather actually covering part of the embroidery.

The ravages of wear and time have changed the appearance of this cloak. Many of the coloured skins have faded from their original rather acid tones and although part of a deep border of black lambskin can be seen at the very bottom of the image, most of the wool has decayed and fallen out.

Man's cloak (*suba*) of leather embroidered with silk.
Hungary (possibly from Veszprém),
second half of the 19th century
Given by Lady Worsley-Taylor
T.192-1931

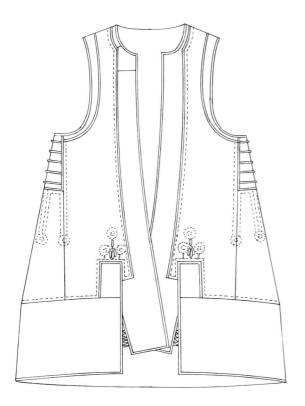

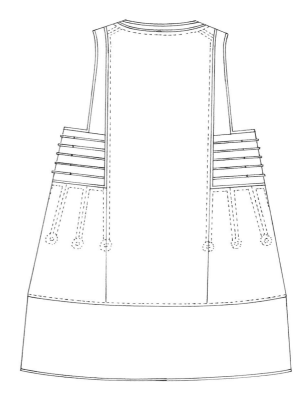

Panels of thick white felt and finer, red felted wool form a striking and bold garment. This has been softened by tiny undulations of red silk cord applied over most of the seams and outlining the finger-like decoration that falls over the hip.

A panel of red wool has been inserted under the arm – possibly because it is more flexible and therefore more comfortable than the white felt – and it has been edged with red and green silk cords.

Five decorative interlaced cords have been placed over this panel and more cords have been twisted into swirls and couched in place. The small roundels are formed by applied pieces of fabric woven with metal threads and bright yellow silk.

More cord can be seen on the drawing where it links the slightly curving front facings with the main garment.

A woman's sleeveless coat of felt and felted wool trimmed with
silk cord and appliqué.
Greece (the Keratea district of Attica), 19th century
Given by A. J. B. Wace
T.720B-1919

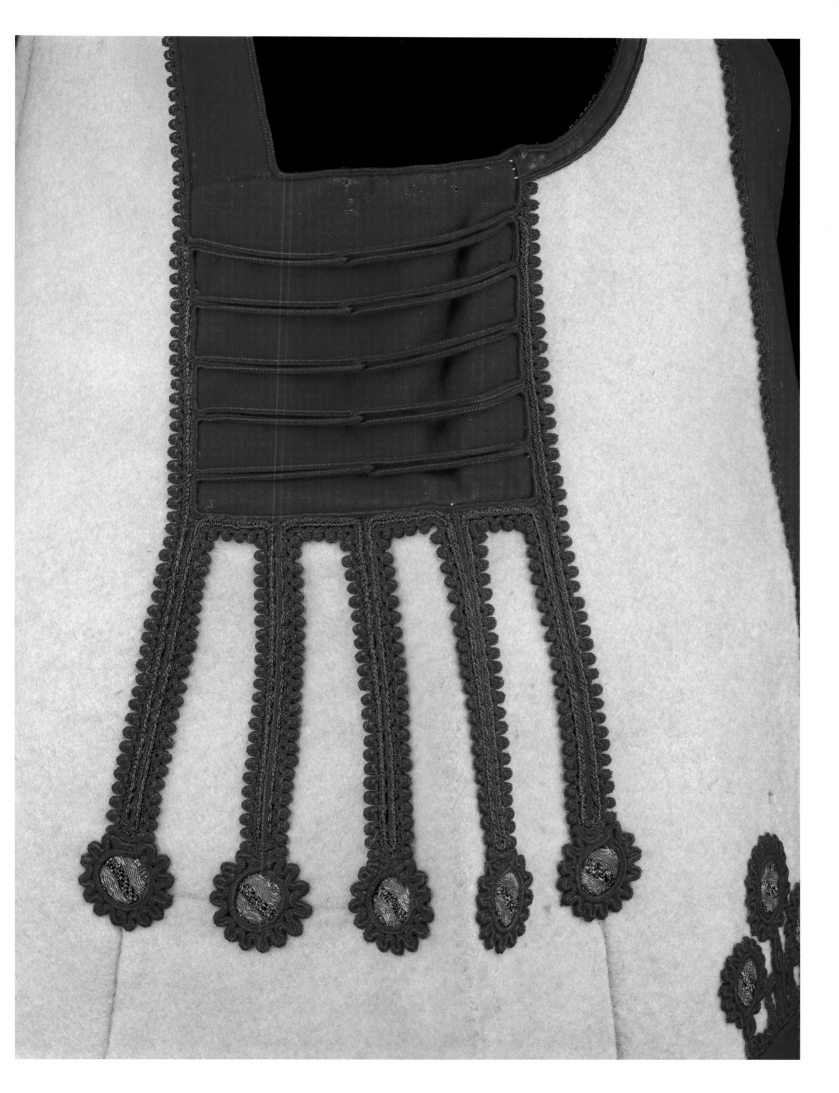

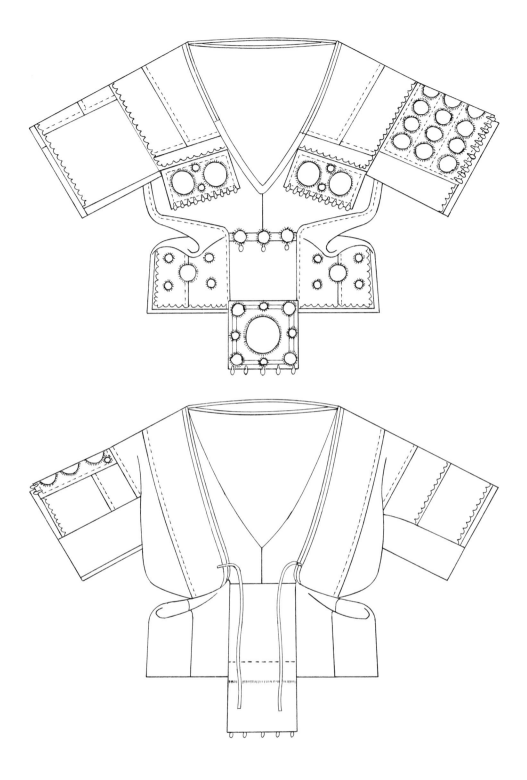

The application of round pieces of mirror-glass to clothing is popular in some parts of India, particularly Rajasthan and Gujarat, and also among the Banjara communities who are spread over large parts of the country. This blouse has two flaps with two large pieces of mirror-glass each on the front, with a further flap with smaller mirrors on each sleeve. The blouse was acquired together with the full skirt, see p.130, which also uses small pieces of mirrorwork on the waistband.

Woman's blouse of cotton and silk fabric with attached mirror-glass.
India (Banjara people, Bidar, Karnataka), early 20th century.
Given by K. de B. Codrington
IM.47a-1933

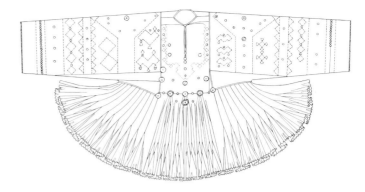

The simple cut of this shirt, in which two rectangles of cloth are sewn together vertically, leaving spaces for the head and the arms, is common to several tribal groups in Burma and elsewhere in South-East Asia, and is used for both male and female dress. This Karen woman's shirt is profusely decorated with silk thread embroidery and with seeds of a type of grass called in English 'Job's Tears' (coix lacryma). It would be worn with a simple tubular skirt. This shirt was collected in the nineteenth century in Burma; the Karen live mainly in the south-east of the country, and also in adjacent parts of Thailand.

Woman's shirt of cotton embroidered with silk thread and seeds.
Myanmar (Burma), (Karen tribe), mid 19th century
6550 (IS)

These plastic and mother-of-pearl buttons are stitched onto the central front panel of a woman's dress, of which the upper front and sleeves are elaborately embroidered and the skirt, while plain, is constructed of a multitude of inserted panels, see p.166. The buttons form a 'zone of transition' at the waist, between the embroidered top section and the plain black skirt beneath. In addition to the buttons, which are purely decorative rather than functional, a Pakistani coin bearing the date 1948 is also stitched below the neck opening. Tiny white beads stitched at intervals around the embroidered section ensure that the dark red embroidery silk stands out against the black ground fabric.

Woman's dress (jumlo) of cotton embroidered with silk thread and decorated with buttons, beads and a coin.
Pakistan (Indus Kohistan, North-West Frontier Province), mid 20th century
IS.33-1996

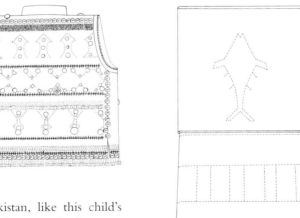

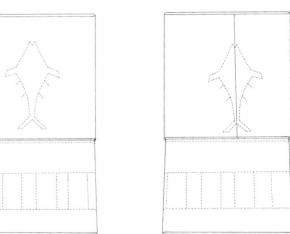

Embroidered garments from northern Pakistan, like this child's waistcoat, are frequently embellished with buttons, zip fasteners, coins, glass beads and metal decorations as well as the fine silk embroidery typical of the region. Like the full-skirted woman's dress (on this page), the ground fabric is a coarse black cotton cloth bought from the nearest bazaar, which may be several days' walk away. The embroidery thread, glass beads and other added decorations would either be bought from the bazaar or from itinerant salesmen who travel throughout these steep valleys branching off from the River Indus.

Child's waistcoat of black cotton fabric, embroidered with silk, and embellished with buttons, glass beads and zip fasteners.
Pakistan (Indus Kohistan, North-West Frontier Province), mid 20th century.
IS.32-1996

The decoration on this tubular dress from Sumba, Indonesia, is arranged so that the fish motif is visible when the upper part of the tube is turned down. This motif is outlined in cut shells, while the lower edge of the dress is patterned with beads, a form of decoration often used on Sumba. This garment also incorporates a strip of ikat-dyed cotton, another technique for which this island is particularly renowned. Ikats from Sumba often depict human figures or animals, especially the horses for which the island is famous.

Woman's tubular dress of cotton, with applied glass beads and shells.
Indonesia (East Sumba), mid 20th century
IS.56-1966

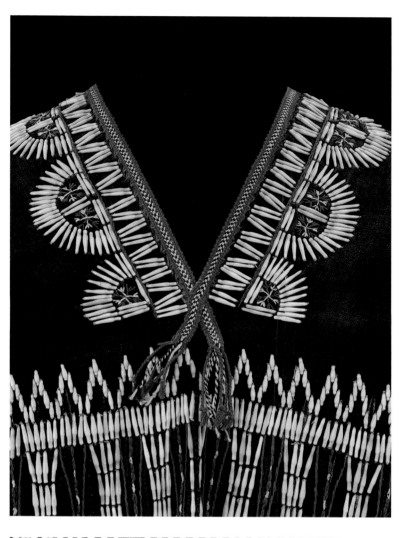

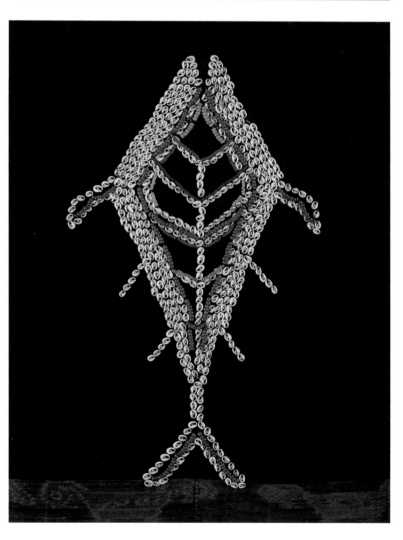

This heavy coat requires no fastenings to keep it in place. Despite this, twenty-two large buttons have been added. Each one is hand-made by winding silk thread around a core, possibly of wood or perhaps a solid pad of fibre. For the final layer a needle has been used to plait metal thread into a pattern.

Each button has been decorated with five beads of coral, considered to be a protection against evil. Sometimes red glass beads are used if coral is too expensive. Considering its relative value it is surprising that the beads are not sewn on individually, instead all five are secured on the same piece of silk thread; when this comes loose all five beads are in danger of being lost.

Woman's coat with hanging sleeves, silk velvet embroidered with metal thread and trimmed with metal braid and cord.
Albania, second half of the 19th century
Given by Lieutenant Colonel C. de S. Luxmoore
T.46-1934

This waistcoat is very stiff because a thin layer of brown cardboard has been inserted between the red felt ground and its silk lining, giving it an armoured feel. The black silk cords have been couched through both the felt and the card.

The physical stiffness is heightened by the use of rigid brass plaques as decoration. Each plaque is flat on one side; there is a small hole at one end through which it has been stitched onto the felt and then concealed beneath the cord edging. Scarlet wool and shiny brass are a military combination in many countries and the unbending character of this garment may have been inspired by such uniforms.

Man's waistcoat of felt, embroidered with silk cord.
Montenegro, late 19th century
Given by George Hubbard
T.181-1928

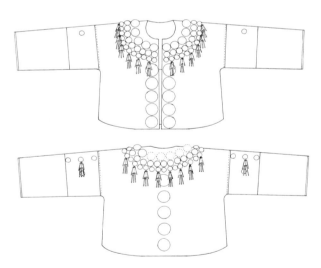

Sight and touch are the senses most associated with dress – we are beguiled by the colours, shapes, textures and movement of what is worn. Sound is seldom associated with dress unless it is the creak of leather or the rustle of silk, but the decorative buttons on this sombre waistcoat are truly musical. Individually they have no sound, but placed closely together they jostle with their neighbour and tinkle and clang like alpine cow bells! Silent, stealthy movement is impossible. They have no function except decoration.

Their smooth, rounded underpart contrasts sharply with the dull coils and chains of wire which cover their top and which encase small shiny beads. The the light which glints from the beads appears to be absorbed by the fine black felt from which the waistcoat is made.

Waistcoat of felt, possibly for a child, embroidered with silk cord and trimmed with metal buttons.
Germany (probably Wurtenburg), c.1870
971-1872

The dramatic silver medallions and pendants that embellish this velvet jacket are used by several related tribal groups in eastern Burma and adjacent parts of northern Thailand. This example is from the Jinghpaw, a sub-group of the large Kachin tribe. Jackets like this would be worn with a woven wrapped skirt, usually of red material, and tall hats of similar fabric, with lacquered cane hoops around the waist.

Woman's jacket of black velvet with applied silver ornaments on front and back.
Myanmar (Burma), (Jinghpaw people, Kachin or Northern Shan State), mid 20th century.
IS.147-1993

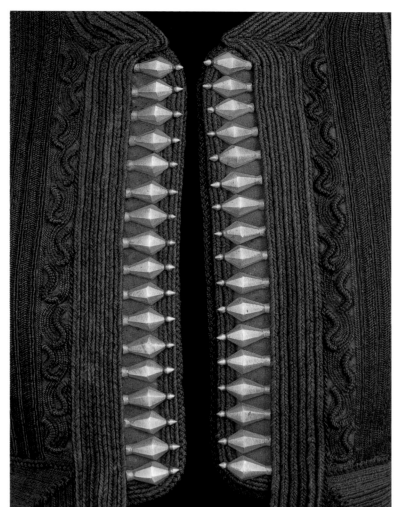

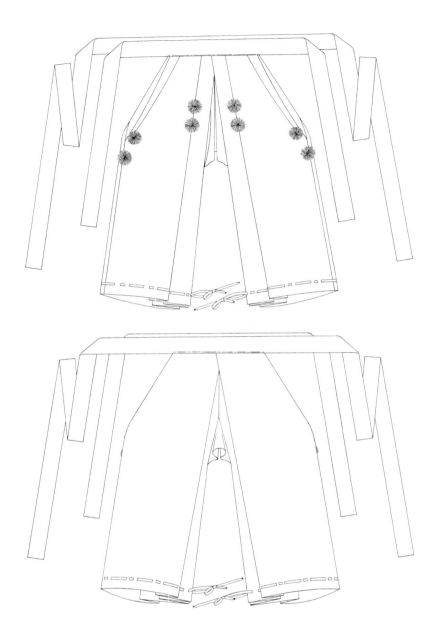

These blue and white pompom-like knots adorn a pair of *hakama*. The wide, pleated trousers, open at the sides and tied at the waist with two pairs of long bands, would have been worn by a *samurai*, a member of the Japanese military class. The knots would have originally helped to reinforce the seams, but by the nineteenth century when this garment was made, they were more decorative than functional. These trousers have a matching jacket and the ensemble is known as a *hitatare*. This particular two-piece outfit may have been designed for wear under armour, the braids at the hem allowing the trousers to be gathered and tucked into boots.

The Edo period (1615–1868) was a time of peace in Japan so there was no opportunity for *samurai* to engage in actual warfare. However, armour would still be worn on ceremonial occasions and when provincial lords marched with their retinue in procession to and from the capital. *Hitatare* were made from rich and elaborately woven fabrics designed to emphasize the *samurai*'s status and enhance the dramatic effect of the whole outfit. This pair of trousers was woven in bright green, purple, red, yellow and cream, but these colours have faded over the years.

Man's trousers (*hakama*) of woven silk
with applied silk knots and braids.
Japan, late 18th – early 19th century
79b-1890

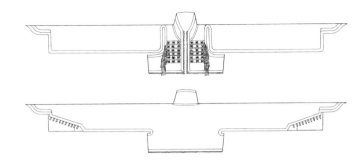

A variety of applied decoration enlivens this satin skirt. Fringes and fancy braids formed into points, scallops and curls surround pleated and padded rosettes of fabric. The reverse is identical to the front. It is a re-worked version of the traditional Chinese woman's skirt (see p.173). Although the decoration on this skirt alludes to the older style, it is not wrapped around the body but put on over the head or pulled up from the feet. From the early decades of the twentieth century, skirts were worn shorter than before, revealing the ankles and unbound feet. Chinese female students, associated with the idea of the 'New Woman' at this period, wore this shorter skirt, often in plain black, with a fitted jacket, usually in white. The socialite version of the same ensemble was much more glamorous. This skirt lies somewhere between the two, being black but also decorated.

Woman's skirt of black satin.
China, 1920s
Valery M. Garrett Collection purchased with funds from the
Friends of the V&A
FE.51-1995

The sleeves of this jacket, lined with pink silk to compliment the purple velvet, are designed to hang from the shoulder down the wearer's back. They are not seamed and open out to reveal their lining. This is a style that found its way into the uniforms of many European cavalry regiments.

The application of braid across the bodice is another feature that has been adopted by the military. These bands have been cut to the correct length and the ends have been folded to form a point, like an envelope, to prevent fraying; the point has then been turned under and stitched in place. Three flowerheads made from different types of wire have been attached to each band; two have been decorated with a large coral bead while a long and intricate wire tassel hangs from the outermost flowerhead.

Woman's short jacket with hanging sleeves, silk velvet embroidered with metal thread.
Bosnia and Herzegovina, 19th century
Given by George Hubbard
T.184-1928

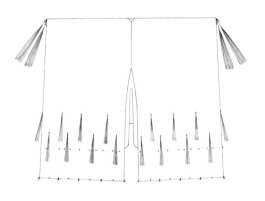

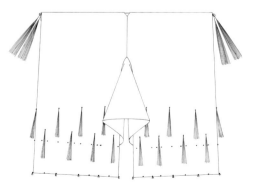

These trousers were part of the costume of a man of the Yinbaw tribe of Kayah State in south-east Burma. They are approximately knee-length and would have been worn with a short, long-sleeved jacket. The narrow cotton tapes, which have been bunched together to form tassels scattered over the lower part of the legs, appear to be of European manufacture.

Man's trousers of cotton with embroidery and attached tassels.
Myanmar (Burma), (Kayah State), early 20th century
IM.152-1929

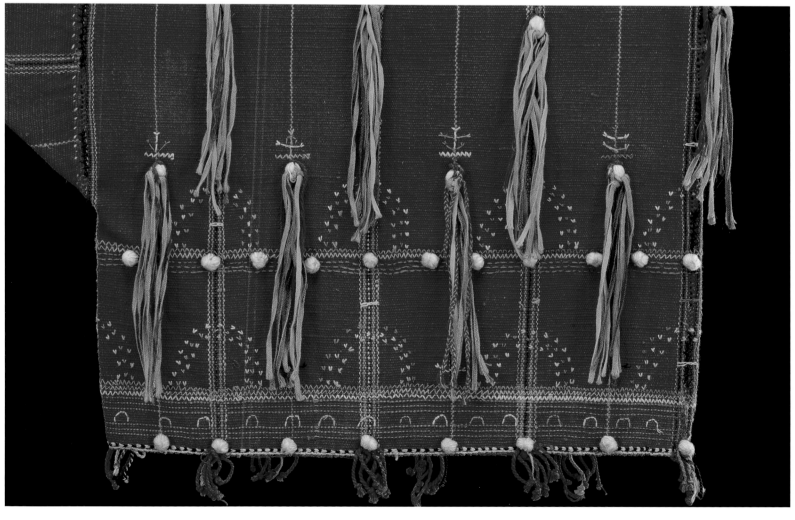

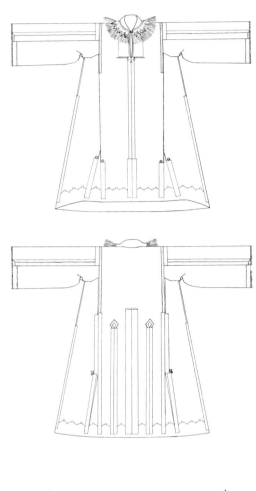

In its first incarnation this dress was made from home-produced materials: hand-woven cotton cloth and hand-spun woollen threads in black and blue. Lines of running stitch join the sleeves to the central panel, the neck slit has been oversewn and three embroidered bands run from it to the hem. A broad embroidered band, in black and blue, runs up either side of the neck slit ending under the thickly fringed cotton collar but, at a later date, more modern facings with a bright flower design have been sewn over the traditional embroidery.

The collar is decorated with short lengths of commercially produced trimmings: facings of fine felt printed with silver, woven braid with an added line of rickrack, a pretty net and crochet edging with an added row of delicate pink glass beads, and, finally, an assortment of odd beads loosely strung so that they hang in clusters.

Woman's dress of cotton embroidered with wool.
Macedonia (Skopska Črnagora near Skopje), 19th century re-trimmed in the early 20th century
Given by Mrs Lucy Duke Kinne
T.264-1990

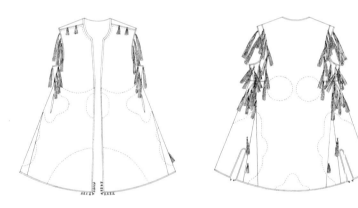

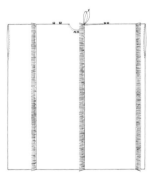

Frivolous tassels and bold embroidery distract the eye from the simple construction of this felt coat. The opening has been bound with blue cloth and two strips of felt – one red and one blue – have been sewn onto the front panel and then it has been covered with silk and cotton embroidery.

The shoulder seam and the armholes have been trimmed with dark brown woollen cords around which red and dark red tassels have been knotted. The longer ones, 15cm (6 inches), are around the armhole and the shorter ones, 8cm (3 inches), are along the shoulder and some of them have been threaded through red and white glass beads. The wool used for the tassels had been very tightly spun so that each thread coils back along its own length creating a wild, untamed mane of colour and movement.

Woman's sleeveless coat of felt embroidered with wool and trimmed with woollen tassels.
Macedonia (Bitolj), 19th century
T.42-1927

This simple garment is made from a horizontal length of cotton, which has been seamed across the shoulders and down one side. What appear as self-coloured vertical stripes in the finished robe were formed by varying thicknesses of weft. In addition there are three patterned bands of coloured silk.

The neck opening is small but extends as a slit along one shoulder and is secured by a yellow and green woollen cord. There are four tiny silk tassels in the centre of the neck which have tangled to form a pompom. The fringing is made with white and red cotton knotted in alternate directions around groups of warp threads as the fabric was being woven; the alternate directions create a wavy effect along each row when the garment is worn.

Man's robe of striped cotton embroidered with silk and trimmed with added cotton fringes.
North Africa (probably Tunisia), late 19th century
Given by Sir Harold E. Stone KCMG, OBE
T.16-1967

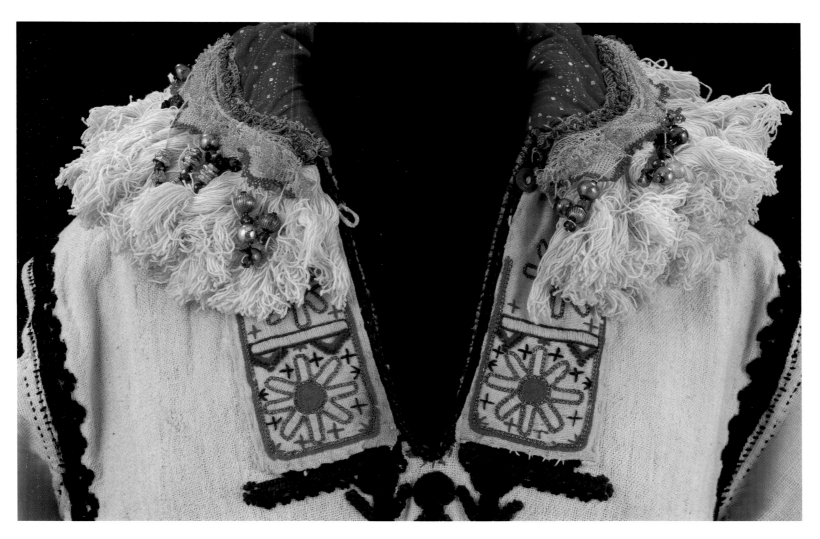

A wealth of embellishments adorn this skirt of red patterned silk. Shaped cotton cut-outs applied to the red ground are liberally sprinkled with sequins and outlined with rows of differently coloured rickrack braid. There are hanging decorations in the form of streamers, silk fringes, strings of plastic pearls ending in bright pink wool tassels and dangling silver bells. The skirt presents a beautiful spectacle but, more than that, when worn and in motion, it would emit rustling and ringing sounds to add to the overall pleasurable effect. Very bright, bold blocks of colour are the hallmarks of festival clothes like this. Such clothing provides a sharp contrast to the workaday garments worn by the Hoklo people, originally boat dwellers of South China who made their living by fishing. This skirt is part of a bridal costume. The type of jacket that went with it can be seen on p.55. To save time, money and material – all-important considerations for these people – the skirt is only decorated in those areas that will show beneath the long jacket. Women who attend the bride also wear a fancy collar and apron similarly decorated. They perform a dragon boat dance in imitation of the groom's original journey by boat to fetch his bride.

Woman's skirt of decorated silk, cotton and wool.
China (Hoklo people), *c*.1980
Valery M. Garrett Collection purchased with funds
from the Friends of the V&A
FE.198-1995

Glossary

ANGARKHA: a type of Indian robe characterized by a circular panel at the neck.

APPLIED/APPLIQUÉ: a decorative technique in which the pattern is formed by sewing pieces of one fabric onto another.

BLACKWORK: embroidery using only black threads.

CHEONGSAM: a fitted dress worn by Chinese women from the late 1920s.

CLOUD COLLAR: a Central Asian form of decoration around the neck and shoulders of a garment.

COUCHING: an embroidery technique in which threads are brought from the back of the fabric, laid in position on the right side and secured with small stitches worked with either similar or contrasting thread.

CURLICUE: a decorative curl or twist.

CUTWORK: a technique used to change the structure of a fabric by removing small areas of it. These spaces are sometimes in-filled with decorative stitching.

DIE: a sharp-edged metal stamp used for cutting.

EYELET EMBROIDERY: eyelets are small holes edged with stitching. They can be isolated or grouped together to form a pattern.

FACING: a lining used on a curved or irregularly shaped area of a garment, such as the neckline or cuffs.

FLOSS SILK: untwisted silk thread.

FROGGINGS: decorative fastenings.

GOTA: a type of ribbon, used in India, woven from silk threads and metallic strips. Often used as applied decoration.

IKAT: a fabric in which the pattern is resist-dyed on the yarn before weaving commences.

INDIGO: a natural blue dye derived from the leaves of plants of the genus *Indigofera*.

INTERLACING STITCH: an embroidery stitch used in Pakistan and western India in which the needle is used to create a basket-like pattern in thread on the surface of the cloth.

KASURI: Japanese term for thread-resist dyeing, similar to ikat.

KESI: Chinese silk tapestry weaving.

LAPPET: a long piece of cloth used to tie a garment.

MADDER: a natural red dye made from the roots of the *Rubia tinctorum* plant.

MITRE: a join between two pieces of braid laid at an angle of 90° so that the bisecting angle is 45°.

MORDANT: a metallic salt needed to fix some natural dyes.

NEEDLELACE: generic term covering all forms of openwork made stitch-by-stitch with a needle and thread.

OPENWORK: an embroidery technique in which the ground threads are either removed or pulled and secured together to form a mesh-like structure.

PATTERN DARNING: running stitches worked in a regular sequence to form a simple repeating pattern.

PLUSH: a woven fabric with a very long pile.

RESIST DYEING: colouring or patterning of a fabric or the yarns for a fabric by blocking off patterned areas with a resist agent – often wax or paste – that prevents these areas from taking the dye. The resist agent is then removed. By repeating this process a multi-coloured pattern can be created.

RICKRACK: a flat woven braid made in a zigzag form.

SILVER STRIP: a very thin and flat ribbon of metal, which can be used as a thread in weaving and embroidery.

SLUB SILK: silk fabric with an uneven texture.

SPRANG: a technique of manipulating taut warp threads to make a patterned, stretchy textile.

TABLET-WOVEN: a narrow fabric woven by using cards, or tablets, instead of the usual shedding devices on looms.

TASAR SILK (also known as tussah or tussore): an Indian wild silk from the undomesticated *Antheraea paphia* silkworm.

WHITEWORK: embroidery using only white or off-white threads.

ZARDOZI: a type of Indian embroidery using gold-wrapped silk thread or gilt silver strips.

Further Reading

Asian Costumes and Textiles: From the Bosphorus to Fujiyama: The Zaira and Marcel Mis Collection (Milan, Skira 2001)

Askari, Nasreen and Crill, Rosemary. *Colours of the Indus: Costume & Textiles of Pakistan* (London, V&A Museum and Merrell Holberton 1997)

Calasibetta, Charlotte Mankey. *Fairchild's Dictionary of Fashion* (New York, Fairchild Publications second edition 1988)

Goswamy, B.N. *Indian Costumes in the Collection of the Calico Museum of Textiles* (Ahmedabad 1993)

Jackson, Anna. *Japanese Country Textiles,* (London, V&A Museum 1997)

Kennett, Frances. *World Dress. A Comprehensive Guide to the Folk Costume of the World* (London, Mitchell Beazley 1994)

Kumar, Ritu. *Costumes & Textiles of Royal India* (London, Christies 1999)

Lynton, Linda. *The Sari* (London, Thames & Hudson 1995)

Maruyama, Nobuhiko. *Clothes of the Samurai Warrior* (Kyoto, Kyoto Shoin 1994)

Maxwell, Robyn. *Textiles of South-East Asia. Tradition, Trade and Transformation* (Melbourne, Oxford University Press 1990)

Roberts, Claire and Huh Dong-hwa. (editors) *Rapt in Colour: Korean Textiles and Costumes of the Chosŏn Dynasty* (Sydney, Powerhouse Museum and The Museum of Korean Embroidery 1998)

Tilke, Max. *The Costumes of Eastern Europe* (London, Ernest Benn 1926)

Tilke, Max. *Costume Patterns and Designs* (New York, Rizzoli 1990)

Wilson, Verity. *Chinese Dress* (London, V&A Museum 1986)

Wingate, Isabel B. *Fairchild's Dictionary of Textiles* (New York, Fairchild Publications sixth edition 1979)

Woodson, Yoko *et al. Four Centuries of Fashion: Classical Kimono from the Kyoto National Museum* (San Francisco, The Asian Art Museum of San Francisco 1997)

SIBERIA

RUSSIA

URAL MOUNTAINS

MONGOLIA

MANCHURIA

UZBEKISTAN

PACIFIC

TAJIKISTAN   XINJIANG

TURKEY

Beijing •

NORTH
KOREA

HOKKAIDO

CHINA

• Pyongyang

JAPAN

OCEAN

• Seoul

SOUTH
KOREA

IRAN

AFGHANISTAN

KASHMIR

TIBET

• Tokyo

Galilee •

• Kandahar

• Lhasa

Lahore •

PANJAB

NEPAL

Shanghai •

The Persian Gulf

PAKISTAN

Delhi •

• Kathmandu

Lucknow •

KACHIN

• Hong
Kong

GUJARAT

INDIA

• Mandalay

DECCAN

MYANMAR
(BURMA)

PHILIPPINES

Bidar •

KARNATAKA

THAILAND

ETHIOPIA

MINDANAO

INDIAN

TRENGGANU

MALAYSIA

SUMATRA

BORNEO

OCEAN

JAVA

INDONESIA

SUMBA

SOUTHERN OCEAN

Index of People and Places